FIGURING IT OUT AS I GO

A JOURNEY INTO THE FATHER'S HEART

by
JEFF LYLE

Dedicated to Amy, the woman whose depth I have never figured out, and I likely will never be able to do so. The joy of being married to you is what I have discovered in trying to figure you out.
You are a beautiful mystery to me, and the single greatest gift God has ever blessed me with after saving me.
You are my favorite.

Dedicated to my two children, Alicia and Landon, Wonder and Thunder, whom I love with deep ache in spite of all my stumbling attempts to convey that to you both: you two are so worth me pursuing and I intend to do so for as long as I live.

Dedicated to King Jesus who found me in helplessness and committed to always keep showing me the way.
I love You, and my desire is that what this book contains will bring pleasure to Your heart.

ACKNOWLEDGMENTS

So many people leap to my mind when it comes to acknowledging partners in ministry who helped bring this book to pass. While many gave perfectly timed encouragement along the way, the following were specifically used by the Father to motivate me to complete this project.

Chad Norris, you prophesied over me that I would one day put my story to print. You called out my destiny in a long season where many other men were speaking death over me. You gave me a holy glare at a restaurant in Greenville one night as you warned me that I would miss the anointing for writing this book if I waited too much longer. Thank you for that swift kick in the pants. You poured Kingdom into me and then set me free to walk out my calling. Thank you, my friend.

Billy Humphrey, you model for me what it means to love Jesus more than I love anyone or anything else. You reinforced to me that ministry is a terrible god and declared over me often that my soul wanted intimacy more than it hungered for any further accomplishments. You make me want to live with an intentional passion that brings everything back to the feet of our King. Thank you, my friend.

Dustin Pennington, you have an anointing for relationships that I will likely never have. Honestly, you amaze me with your seemingly effortless interaction with people. You taught me the lost art of a positive outlook and always believing for the best. Apart from you listening to the Holy Spirit, I'm unsure where I would be today in Kingdom ministry. I so enjoy watching you flow with people. You have helped me immeasurably to remember how not to lose sight of the individual sheep while advancing the entire flock. Thank you, my friend.

Art and Cleveland Gaynor, what a treasure you are to me! God, in omniscient wisdom, knew what was lacking in major places in my life. He sent you as ambassadors of help to shore up some of those things so that my ship kept sailing. To this day, you two are the most precious fruit that has been born from Transforming Truth. More than fruit, you are my friends. I thank God for you both. Without you coming alongside of the Lyles, this book would have never found a convenient season to be written. May the Lord richly reward you for your investments in me.

Jennifer Woodruff and Jill Rakestraw, I cannot believe you two have hung in there with me for all these years. Jen, your commitment to Jesus and proficiency in managing the daily needs of Transforming Truth have secured you great reward in Heaven. I am convinced of this. Your servant heartedness will never be forgotten by me. You have the spirit of an overcomer. Jill, you proofread and helped edit this manuscript while you were immobilized after a surgery – who does that?! You fixed all of my terrible punctuation and made it appear that I am actually an educated man. You are a faithful and detailed daughter of God who thirsts for excellence in everything. I am so grateful for you. Thank you, my two sisters and friends.

To all those whom I have led and served at Meadow, New Bridge, and IHOP Atlanta, much of this book reveals what God taught me through you. In times of blessing and seasons of burden, you were the instruments of His instruction to me. I love all of you – even the ones who caused me pain. To those of you who felt pain from me, I am so sorry. I trust that His grace has touched the wounds that I caused and that there was something beautiful placed inside any hole I dug in you. I make no excuses, and I hope that your memories of me are as Gospel-insulated as mine are of you. I love the assurance that we will all be best friends again in Heaven. Grace to each of you!

TABLE OF CONTENTS

PREFACE

I am in Kansas City right now with about two hundred people sitting scattered throughout a room, most of them with their eyes closed, or their hands raised, or their heads bowed. There is a middle-aged man with an unapologetic New York accent, wearing a Yankees cap, praying rhythmically on a microphone. On the platform behind him are eight young millennials playing instruments, moving in and out of singing spontaneously unto Jesus. There is a thickening presence of God in the room as the man on the mic declares in increasing volume, "You are still amazing to me, Jesus… We just want to say to You, 'Thank You!'…We could not even be here apart from You, so give us courage to continue to declare Your name! There is nobody like You, Lord! Nobody!"

I have been in many similar settings over the years. Potent, palpable, presiding Heavenly presence takes ownership of the room. *God is here.* I cannot see Him, but it is no loss to me – He is in this little place with us. It is striking me anew: **I am in a room with the Almighty.**

> *How did a once-abandoned, perpetually frightened eight-year-old end up in this room as a man now nearing fifty years old?*
>
> *Is it even remotely conceivable that a miserable, raging teenage drunk could find himself sitting here in this vibrant worship scene so many years later?*
>
> *What force could have possibly brought into this Holy Spirit-ruled room a formerly young man in his early twenties who was addicted to his darkness? What is it that transformed him so that he would be sitting among these worshipers in Missouri, wiping the tears off his face as the singers begin to worship an invisible King in antiphonal praise?*

The answers to the questions above, and many more about my journey – and some answers that you may have discovered about your own life – are the reasons that I am writing this book. I have a simple goal in mind.

My aim is to point, re-point, repeatedly point, and *uber-point* all of us back to a tighter orbit around this beautiful and glorious king named Jesus, and toward His throne of love and grace. Some time back, He nudged me to write down my story. I squirmed against the nudge. It got firmer. I pulled away a bit farther and hoped to remain distracted from the assignment He was calling me to embrace. He even sent a prophetic man, full of grace and grit, to say to me, "The Father wants you to write that book. Wait too much longer, and you will be tardy for the anointing to get it done." Not long after that, in loving authority, I felt God's grasp and heard Him whisper to my heart, "Do it, Jeff. It is not a request, son." Funny, it was that firm whisper that freed me up to begin to tell you about how God has led me, through years full of unusual twists and turns, more fully into Himself. So, here I am writing the book.

This is my story. This is my song. What follows are my *life-lyrics,* and if I do what I am supposed to do, you will be strengthened by this tale that I am going to share.

That little boy, frightened and feeling abandoned, *was me.* That raging adolescent who put on his own chains that would weigh him down for a very long, smothering decade was me. That young, soul-darkened man in his early twenties was me. If God was taken out of the equation, I would not be here to write a single word of this story. There wouldn't be a story — just another unrecorded tragedy. None of what I have written or will write in this book is exaggerated. The bad was as bad as I will reveal it to be. The good has been even better than I reveal it, simply because my vocabulary is not sufficient to convey the treasures of the Father's love, grace, and mercy to me.

This is a story about **Jesus**. I am in the story, so in that sense, it is my story, but I am not the central figure within it. This is a story about overcoming. It's all about a grand reversal, gifted to me through God's grace, which led to countless more successive reversals in my life. This is one man's account about how a patient, gracious, and amazing Father moved him from being

a **rebel** to being **redeemed**, to temporarily becoming pitifully **religious**...
only later to know the exhilaration of being fully **released** into the freedom
provided to all Christians in the Holy Spirit.

When I asked the Lord why He wanted my first book to be about my
personal story, His answer both humbled me and liberated me. He said to
me, "It's really not your story, son. It is Mine. I just wrote it with your life.
You are in it, Jeff, but it is all about Me. Just start writing; you will see it's
about Me, and so will those who read your words."

So, let me tell you about my journey to find the Father's heart. He is the
Author of my story. I am hoping that in reading this, you will deeply
connect or reconnect with the story that the Father is writing with your —
own life. There are still more chapters to come for both you and me. As for —
me, I am always figuring it out as I go.

February 16, 2019
Kansas City, Missouri, USA

SECTION 1

BEFORE HIM

CHAPTER 1

A Struggler from the Start

"Before I formed you in the womb I knew you, and
before you were born I consecrated you..."
- Jeremiah 1:5

SOMEWHERE AROUND 4:00 A.M. ON Tuesday, the sixteenth of June in 1970, a twenty-four-year-old woman in Miami gave birth to her second child – a son. When my mother, Karen, emerged victorious from a twenty-five-hour labor with a stubborn baby boy, relief found her a couple of hours before the Florida sunrise did. Mom would remind me more than once during my life how hard it was bringing me into this world. When all was said and done, she and my dad would leave the birthing wing of the hospital on Homestead Air Force Base with their almost three-year-old daughter, Stephanie, and her new baby brother whom they had named Jeffrey. Five months after I was born, Staff Sergeant Cary Douglas Lyle finished his time in the military during the Vietnam War and moved his little family back to the place of his roots in Atlanta, Georgia. Settled back in my dad's hometown, boxes were unpacked by the time my very first Christmas arrived. Dad and mom began another chapter of change in their young marriage. By both of their admissions, they were *marital misfits* together. Like so many young married couples both then and now, realities about adulthood, marriage, and parenthood were already throwing them curveballs that they were ill-equipped to hit. I can tell you that my very early years never left me feeling anything other than loved by both of them. They were two flawed people doing the best that they could. Looking back, I recognize now that we were pretty poor. I never felt it though – my earliest days were happy. Both sets of grandparents were integrated into our lives along with aunts, uncles, and cousins. Like most children who are far too young to grasp the world of adults, I had no idea of the struggles and pains that my parents were living with as both of their weaknesses served their marriage like frayed wires that occasionally smoked, sparked, and smoldered.

Around the time I was migrating toward preschool age, my world of blissful ignorance was removed forever. My guess is that the marital tensions had reached a boiling point. I don't remember any yelling or commotion right before *the moment* occurred. What I do remember is that long-ago day when my father moved swiftly past me where I sat on the floor of our den. I remember him yanking the front door open and slamming it behind him. I never saw my dad angry before that day. I stood up just in time to see him backfist the window on his way down the sidewalk. The glass shattered inward where I was now standing in the den, and some of it landed right in front of me. Though I would not recognize it for many years, something more than the window got shattered that day. Also broken was my sense of security that small children often draw from their sense of a healthy family unit. My mom was suddenly there as my dad hastily got into his car, and she whisked me up into her arms so that I didn't step in any of the glass. As she held me in her arms, I saw my dad aggressively back out of the driveway in his old Chevy Nova and roar up the street. That's all I remember about that day. Dad was going to be gone for a while. Not an hour or a day or a week. The best I can remember, he moved out, and a short time later, he and mom were divorced. What is strange to me, as I recall that season in our lives, is that I only have snapshot memories of it all. It's not like a high-definition video memory – just a series of still-shots that hold the contents of an uncomfortable story. I think dad was gone somewhere between a year or two, and Stephanie and I would get to be with him on weekends. I remember his apartment. I remember sleeping on a sofa bed with my seven-year-old sister during our visits. I remember going swimming in the pool at the apartment complex and learning how to have fun again. Other than that, there is only that convenient memory-fog that likely protects young hearts from the complexities that their parents face. What is amazing is that this particular season had an extremely unexpected end. Yes, this chapter had an unforeseen twist. You see, *dad came back home to us.* Doug and Karen Lyle humbled themselves and, likely for the sake of their kids, made another go at marriage with one another. There was a quaint re-marriage ceremony as the Father presented all of the Lyles with an opportunity for a relational reset.

I don't remember anything other than us suddenly becoming a foursome again. We started over, and I so admire my parents for doing what likely felt like a doomed do-over from the restart. They sought to stand firm for our family. They hungered and thirsted for what was right. They knew it would cost them, but they did what they believed was best. Eventually, right around my seventh birthday, we moved into the suburbs of Atlanta into a little house in Lilburn, Georgia. We were a family again, and I felt hopeful in what I assumed would be the permanence of a new season of life. Lilburn would be the city of the longest span of my childhood years. It was also the scene of the most painful event that ever found me. This city would be the setting of the chapter that significantly shaped who I would be for nearly twenty years which followed.

It will be hard for me to write it, and it may even be difficult for you to read some of it, but the brilliance of the eventual diamond that would come forth shines best against the black backcloth. So, let me begin to unfold some of that dark cloth for you.

CHAPTER 2

Emotionally Mugged at Too Young an Age

"His children are far from safety; they are crushed in the gate, and there is no one to deliver them."
– Job 5:4

LIVING IN LILBURN WAS BEAUTIFUL at the beginning. Right after second grade started, my parents signed me up to play soccer. I was a runt – short, skinny, all knees, attached to stubby little legs. My mom's side of the family is on the smaller side, while my dad's people had always been of average build. I got a heavier dose of my mom's DNA, and I basically spent my childhood looking like a perpetually fasting leprechaun. My mother, who was being influenced heavily by the Women's Liberation movement that had taken the nation by storm at that time, agreed to be the team mom for my soccer team, bringing drinks and snacks to thankless little boys practice after practice, game after game. Later on in life, she would tell me how this short season as a soccer mom played a pivotal role in her growing identity crisis at that time. Soccer turned out to not be my thing, so my parents then enrolled me in the local baseball league for boys. Again, mom helped out with cookies, Cokes, and cups as any dutiful team mom does. Dad was always at my games, cheering me on as I got walked on four pitches nearly every time I came to the plate (it was hard for my opponents to throw strikes to a pint-sized suburbanite hobbit). I literally never swung the bat that first year of baseball. Not one swing. I walked every time or got called out on non-swinging strikes. My performances were less than exhilarating. The next year, I was promoted up to an older age-group where I learned quickly that they knew how to throw strikes. Those older kids struck me out nearly every time. Two years into my baseball career, I still had never gotten a base hit. Even as an eight-year-old, an American male has an ego. I felt pretty awful about myself. Short, skinny, batting in the last slot in every single game, I wanted to quit, but my dad was wise to have me fulfill my commitment to the team to finish the season. At the end of the last game of my second Little League season, Coach McCormick gave us a rally speech that rang hollow to my young ears. It was more than just baseball that was dragging down my spirits. I recognize now that something *atmospheric* was going on in my family life. Mom was growing increasingly unhappy and pulling away from dad. My parents' marriage was fraying behind the scenes, and a consequent sadness was touching all of our lives there on Renee Court — in Lilburn. I couldn't identify it, but there was a corrosive spirit that was at work all around us. Whatever it was, it had also started to get *inside* of me.

Looking back at that time, I realize now that there were also spiritual forces swirling about my family that were about to crash upon the shore. Scripture depicts Satan as a hungry lion, roaming around looking for someone to consume. In our family, that predatory lion had sniffed something out that appealed to his appetites. He had strategized to make a meal out of the Lyles, and the Hell's dinner bell was ringing loudly in Lilburn, Georgia. One evening, when I was about eight years old, my father asked me to come into the family room. I still remember his words as he stood in the doorway of my bedroom at the end of the hall:

"Your mother has something she needs to tell you."

I just now felt *it* trying to creep back up in me again as I typed that last sentence. The human mind and emotions are so unfathomable. I am nearly fifty years old as I am typing this, but I literally had five seconds of a young boy's dread just crawl up my throat as I remembered walking from my bedroom across the parquet wood floor by our front door and onto the 1970s burnt-orange carpet of our family room. My mom was sitting on the couch. My dad was sitting in an armchair. He said it again, "Your mother wants to tell you something, son."

It is probably important to say that, at that point in my young life, I felt much closer to my mother than I did my father. That is fairly typical for that stage in a young boy's life. Naturally, I sat down close to my mom on the sofa, and although I cannot remember her exact words, I do remember her telling me

7

that she needed to leave us and our home in Lilburn. I remember looking at my father at that moment and his face was somewhere between stoic and incredulous that my mom was actually having this devastating conversation with me. My older sister was not in the room with us, as they had told her the bad news earlier in the day, so, not surprisingly, she was in her bedroom processing the implosion that had found our family that day. Mom was still talking, but I was not hearing much more of anything that was coming out of her mouth. I zeroed in on her saying that she was unhappy in Lilburn and that she needed to *go and try to find herself*. Eight-year-olds do not know what that phrase means. The whole conversation likely lasted around five minutes before, at some point, I jumped up off the couch and began running to my bedroom. **I would not stop that instinctual fear-fueled running away for a very long time.** I recall slamming my open hand against the wood-paneled wall in our family room as I stormed out of the place where my childhood nightmare was unfolding. It was in that very moment that raging hurt took full occupancy of my heart. It was not a conscious decision on my part to give way to that tyrannical emotion of rage. It simply came upon me with brute force, and I became its prisoner. I choose my wording carefully here when I write that; at that moment, I was emotionally raped by the unpredictability of life. Sadly, that resultant, perpetual movement in and out of rage and sadness would dominate me for the next sixteen years. Most seeds take a little time to germinate. Not this one. As soon as it rooted down in my little-boy heart that day, it began bearing instant fruit. *Bad fruit. Rotten fruit.* It became like Georgia kudzu in my soul that grew at its own pace, in every direction, and without any boundaries being honored. I became a tangled soul.

Looking back, I am not sure there was much I could have done to stop the pain and rage at that juncture in my life. Simply put, children do not have the capacity to safely process life tsunamis that crash in and change the coastline of their hearts. Mom was doing what she felt she needed to do. Dad could not stop her. I felt powerless, isolated, and rejected. There was something that seemed much more *wrong* to me about a mother – my mother – leaving her children than a father leaving them. Moms were never supposed to leave. Moms provided the care. Moms brought the heart to homes. Mama bears were supposed to fight to the death for their little cubs. Moms did not make announcements about going away to find themselves. Moms did not take half the furniture away in a U-Haul on a weekend while dads took the kids to a movie. Moms were not supposed to forward their mail to a new city, *but my mom did...* and it crunched up all my insides. It will not be until I receive a glorified understanding in Heaven that I will be able to fully grasp what all shifted within my soul that day. I am convinced that my mom felt like she was entirely out of all other reasonable options. I cannot begin to understand what emotional and marital weight she was processing at the time of my parents second divorce. There is no way she could have anticipated what her decision would do to her children. After all, ours was certainly not the first family nor the last to be splintered by divorce. There was so much surrounding our family dynamics at that time that I could not fathom it then and I do not pretend to grasp it now. All I know is that, to this very day, mom leaving us was the single most painful event that I have ever experienced.

By the immeasurable grace of God, however, the pain would ultimately be made into the surprisingly glorious platform from which I dove headlong into a pool of redemption, mercy, and hope. **What the enemy of my soul meant for evil, King Jesus would harness for my greatest good.** That aforementioned hungry lion had certainly bitten me, but he would not be permitted to swallow me.

Between that day of bad tidings in the family room in Lilburn and the moment of my eventual redemption in a bedroom in Lawrenceville, there would be a long, deep, dark valley of my own making. I am going to take you through that undesirable valley with me on the beginning pages of this book. I won't stop at every high cliff, pause to recount every cold, tormented night, or become *re-petrified* in the presence of every wild beast that found me there, but I will share enough to let you know just how hard I ran in the wrong direction. Why would I share any of this?

Because it is the bad news that makes the good news good.

9

CHAPTER 3
Pain Management

"The purpose in a man's heart is like deep water,
but a man of understanding will draw it out."
– Proverbs 20:5

I AM A JESUS FOLLOWER. Later in this book, I will share with you how that came to be. When my mom and dad divorced, I was not yet saved. I was not a true Christian yet. While they were together, my parents did what most parents did in the 1970s in Atlanta. Part of the culture back then was that we were expected to pledge allegiance to the Bible-belt norms of going to church, reading the Good Book, and embracing a moral code that found some sort of moorings in the ways of God as prescribed by Southern evangelicals. For whatever reason, for all of us Lyles, the attempt to assimilate into this cultural expectation was a bit of a misfire. We were all nonconformists – even my sister and me at our young ages. Truth be known, mom was a budding liberal and dad was an unapologetic conservative. My guess is that Gloria Steinem and *Cosmo* may have been influencing mom more than the words of Jesus Christ or the Apostle Paul during that time. Traditional, cultural Christian norms just weren't going to be our thing.

Our house sat in a cul-de-sac, and one of our neighbors there on Renee Court was a Roman Catholic woman from Maryland who was fiercely pro-life. She and my mom had some feisty debates about freedom of choice versus right to life before mom moved away. Two doors down on the other side of Renee Court was an outspoken Pentecostal lady who rubbed mom wrongly from the very get-go with her *holy-roller* perspective on life and womanhood. Looking back, I wonder if these two women might have been sovereignly positioned by the Father on each side of my mom for a couple of years in an effort to help her through her burgeoning identity crisis. Regardless of whether or not there was some divine strategy behind where our house was situated, there was zero shifting of mom's political and cultural views. She had become an unapologetic feminist who was suffocating under the pressures to conform to the suburban expectations of what it meant to be a woman in the late 1970s. The storm continued to develop within her troubled heart. Having gone through my own major shifts in cultural views and deciding who I am as a man, I can empathize today with the conflict that she must have been carrying within back then. *Becoming* is often an inwardly violent process.

Please know that my mom was conflicted but still engaged with her children. Like the majority of parents, she loved us with an imperfect love. While I wish now that she had possessed greater discretion in the views which she exposed us to as children, apart from my mother's influence, I would not be writing this book today. She imparted to me a love for words. She, with a little help from Sesame Street, taught me to read well by age four, and she constantly gave me books all the way up through the early days of my Christian journey. Mom was a dreamer, and any creativity I possess should likely be credited to her. One of my concerns in writing some of the raw realities contained in my story is that people might view my mother exclusively as a woman who left her son. **There was way more to her than that.** Yet, for me, there is, sadly, no greater context in which I have ever been able to view her. Mom was intelligent, funny, a lover of music, over-the-top artsy, and a bit of a bohemian released a little too late in time. It is wise for me to never reduce her comprehensive identity down to *who she was to me*. In the end, I really do believe she tried her best. I still remember her reason for leaving was to go and find herself. I am unsure that she ever actually succeeded in her quest. My sincere hope is that she truly did.

Though I was not a Christian as a child, I was blessed to be exposed to the Gospel of Jesus by both of my parents, and also by a precious family there in our Lilburn neighborhood. Had I been a believer in those days, I surely would have been better equipped to deal with the pain that dominated me when my parents split. Frankly, I just had no ability to manage the hurt and rage, so I did what so many others do: **I stuffed it deep down**. I found an incredibly accessible but wholly insufficient, tragically unsuccessful way to manage my hurt. What was it? I pretended that I was fine. I muzzled my little-boy groans and hoped that they would leave me. As you might expect, my approach was an epic failure. Lava doesn't disappear in the absence of a volcanic eruption. *It just bubbles and waits.*

Pain management is a multilaned road to travel. My wife, Amy, whom I will introduce to you in much detail later, still suffers from chronic pain after a devastating auto-collision that happened in 2011. When she came home from a month in the hospital, during which she submitted to more than a dozen surgical procedures and having been given a discouraging prospect of possible confinement to a wheelchair, the doctors had her taking more than fifteen medications to manage her pain. Her right leg, according to her orthopedic surgeon, was so structurally damaged that it looked like a grenade had gone off inside of it. Initially, they thought they would have to amputate, but this amazing surgeon wanted to see if he could put Mrs. Lyle back together again. When our friends learned of the number of narcotics she was taking after her initial discharge from the hospital, some of them offered unsolicited advice encouraging us to just trust God and pray all of the pain away. *Christians can be downright mindless at times.* One well-intending friend actually suggested acupuncture as her prescribed course of treatment. People mean well, but unless you have undergone a season of unceasing physical pain, and unless your bones and joints have been replaced with rods, screws, and plates, it is best to just offer up compassion and choose to withhold your advice. Within two weeks of coming back home from the hospital, Amy weaned herself cold-turkey off of all but one medication, which she further whittled down to just one-eighth of the recommended dosage from the doctor. She hated the meds, and somehow, she tore off her Fentanyl patch, asked us to flush more than a dozen other prescriptions down the commode, and leaned hard into the Lord during thirty-six hours of intense withdrawal symptoms. The Father freed her up to regain her sense of being herself and out from under the deadening effects of those mind-altering prescription drugs. **Amy is a warrior, and personally, she is the most heroic person I have ever met.** She motivates me. Nowadays, her ongoing pain management comes through heavy measures of God's grace and a pinch of what medical science can provide. She still feels the daily physical discomfort, *but she owns it.* It has never been allowed to own her. Amy Lyle is a boss.

When it comes to the subject of pain management, my own pain was not physical. Instead, I had a deep soul wound and was somewhat left to myself to learn how to cope with it. I am not sure as to why, but I did not feel that I was permitted as a child to express my inner pain to my parents. My dad had become an executive in the banking industry, and he was trying to figure out single-parenthood in the context of a career that was very demanding. I honestly do not think he could have known how isolated I felt at that time. On my alternating weekends with my mother, we just went out and had fun. For a while, my sister and I really enjoyed weekends with mom. We went to movies and restaurants and were granted a no-border openness with her that allowed us to talk about things with a carefree liberality that I did not share with anyone else. She was fun and we were bonding in different ways as I crept close to my teenage years. Mom did, indeed, seem happier away from the *Stepford Wives* scenario she had left behind in Lilburn.

Even at that young age, I assumed responsibility for not adding any sense of guilt to mom for moving away. I lived out that presumed responsibility by not discussing my own emotional struggles about the divorce. I never expressed to her my hurt and anger. Dad and I connected over baseball, not deep conversations about my emotions. Truthfully, I remember feeling extremely alone and constantly afraid of life's potential to ambush me. As I write this, I really want to submit to you again that I think both of my parents were trying to do the best

13

they could. I so love and admire my father for refusing to leave his children behind for a second time. Dad fought for us. He told mom that she could leave him if she must, but the kids would not be going with her. I did not know about any of that detailed background info until I was in my late thirties. My father dug in his heels on behalf of my sister and me. What amazing release found me when that news crystallized in my spirit later as an adult. Yet, for nearly three decades prior, there had just been pain...but there was nobody around me who grasped how to help me manage it rightly.

I was forced to figure it out as I go.

Dad remarried an amazing woman, Claudia, a few years later when I was twelve. Outside of Jesus, she is by far the best thing that ever happened to Doug Lyle. I love her for many reasons, but most of all, because she was the woman my dad always needed. Sadly, when dad and Claudia married, there arrived in my heart a new layer of abandonment that attached itself to the already-anchored layer of hurt from when mom left. It was weird – I was happy for dad, but I interpreted his gain to be yet another loss for me. Their marriage was a package deal for all of us as Claudia had two daughters of her own, Ann and Leslie. Dad and Claudia loved each other, but the four children they now shared were ill-equipped to begin a new life together. Ann and Leslie had to uproot from their lives in a nearby city when they moved into the house in Lilburn. They even had to give up their dog, Babe, shortly after our parents' wedding because we had no good place for her in our newly formed family unit. Stephanie, my older sister, was fifteen by this time and had been *the lady of the house* for three years. That changed in an instant, and Stephanie responded with hurt, resentment, anger, and rebellion. I am not at liberty to share my three sisters' stories, but they, along with their brother, spent the next several years living in varying degrees of brokenness and recklessness. It may sound too simplistic, but because all four children felt like we had been replaced, each of us sought out a new version of family. As with most children looking for a tribe, we picked foolishly. I likely made the worst choices of all four of us in this area. **This was self-prescribed pain management for me.**

> *I became determined not to hurt anymore.*
> *I refused to allow anyone to ever ambush my life again.*
> *The jagged edge of reality had already drawn too much of my blood.*
> *So, to manage my pain, I went into hiding.*
> *Right there in plain sight.*
> *I told myself, "I will just have to figure it out as I go."*

Time began to move quickly for me, and at fourteen years old I remember making a decisive commitment to walk away from a childhood that I felt had robbed me. I decided to start living like a man – or at least what I thought a man to be: decisive, strong, never able to be hurt, and most obviously, intensely driven to conquer. Yet, on the inside, I was still a little boy running away from the pain that I had never learned to manage. No remedy found me. No rescue arose to bring understanding and peace. Like so many others, I just learned to live with the broken shards. Human resilience can be impressive, can't it? If we only knew how many people live daily stuffing the pain, suppressing the bitterness, and caging the fear. It is not healthy, but it is the chosen course of pain management for countless people, both young and old. Nobody wants to embrace the pain. We prefer any of the available numbing agents presented to us.

The next season of my story is the hardest to write. It is hard because there are just some things that should never be written down. So, I won't actually write *those* things. It is also hard because I know that, even as I write what I can, it will unearth some things that I buried under the blood of my Savior a long time ago. I do not like to revisit graves, especially the burial places of my saddest days and darkest sins. It is hard to write about this next season, mostly, because this particular time of my life held the years of *my shame*. I took what happened in my childhood and turned it into something much worse, something it never had to be. Because of my inability to manage (or remedy) the pain of my mother's departure and the disintegration of our family, I angrily swung my razor-sharp machete of bitterness, and I cleared a path straight to the quagmire of my shame.

*The pain led to fear. Fear led to anger and deception. Deception led to fatalism…*and when a teenager becomes fatalistic, he lives convinced that nothing really matters.

And when anyone reaches that regrettable place, there is only a deepening darkness.

SECTION 2
AWAY FROM HIM

CHAPTER 4

Blindly Finding a Tribe

*"Be not quick in your spirit to become angry,
for anger lodges in the heart of fools."*
- Ecclesiastes 7:9

THE FATHER IS REAL. HE is good. He is Holy. He is loving and kind and compassionate and merciful. **I believe all of these things about God.** I also believe that He is *sovereign*. If you are unfamiliar with that term, it simply means that God sits atop the mountain of glory in uncontested authority, ruling and reigning over everything. Yes, God is the One in control. He is intentional and unfathomable in all of His ways. You and I will never fully understand the Father, but that does not mean that we cannot know Him. When you come to a surrendered place of entrusting of yourself to Him, His sovereignty no longer intimidates or unnerves you. When you are convinced that He is good, and also good *on your behalf*, you are able to trust that His sovereign oversight of your life is for your benefit. The Father is truly weaving all things together for the good of those who love Him. As we grow in relationship with Him throughout the various chapters of our lives, we are able to look back and comprehend how He used even the bad things for an ultimately good purpose. The big question that backfists some people right in their soul is why this sovereign Father does not prevent all the pains, losses, and difficulties from occurring in the first place. If He is good, and if He is in full control, why does He not forbid the bad stuff?

I feel that these are legitimate questions if they are asked by us in an honest desire to understand Him better. Most who ask questions like these are not sincerely looking for answers. They are dropping accusations that God has done something wrong by failing to do what they wanted Him to do. The bottom line is that we cannot fully understand all the *why's* of God's ways.

When these issues arose in the mind of the Apostle Paul and those who read his letter to the Christians throughout the ancient Roman Empire, he responded by reorienting their focus off of their present suffering and forward onto their forthcoming deliverance. He wrote in Romans 8:18, "For I consider that the sufferings of this present time are not worth comparing with the glory that is to be revealed to us." It may serve us well to recall that **God the Father did not even spare His own Son, Jesus, from the realities of suffering on earth**. God promises triumph over suffering to those who trust Him. He promises none of us, however, immunity from trouble. He promises deliverance and victory to every single one who endures unto the end with Him, fully resting in His mercy and grace. This is the God in whom I believe – not one who immunizes us from all pain, but one who meets us there in the midst of it.

Yet, with the exact same certainty that I express about the goodness and activity of God, I am convinced equally of the evil and active strategy of Satan, the Father's enemy. By the way, it is not an equal fight. In truth, there is not even a scintilla of the possibility that Satan, that cursed and fallen angel, could ever emerge victorious in the war that he wages against the throne of God. *Lo, his doom is sure.* Scripture declares that Satan operates in a sadistic, hellish violence because he is fully aware that his time is short **(see Revelation 12:12)**. The ticking of Heaven's clock enrages Hell's proud prince. Jesus described Satan as a thief who is committed with an evil agenda to steal, kill, and destroy. The plain teaching of the Bible is that the original source of all loss, pain, death, and suffering is Satan who facilitates sin to become the predominant atmosphere on planet earth. We are taught that Satan has strategies **(see 2nd Corinthians 2:11)**. Scripture also reveals that there is an organizational element to the ranks of demons who operate under his command to perpetuate spiritual darkness on earth **(see Ephesians 6:12)**. While my purpose here is not to give a lengthy explanation of the realm of the demonic, it is of great importance that we all understand that, because Satan hates God and His glory, he has strategized and committed to destroying anything that reveals God's glory in the earth.

Therefore, Satan and his demons *hate people*, those who are made in the image of God, and no version of human life reveals more of the purity, innocence, and love of God than young children. Yes, you understood me correctly: all of the evil, raging, merciless fury of Hell is unapologetically aimed at our children. Fewer things delight Satan more than to steal, kill, and destroy the youngest and most innocent among us.

And that is why he went after me.

That is why he went after you when you were young.

That is why he has stirred such darkness in multiple cultures across the planet whose people demand greater permissions and techniques to exterminate human life in the womb. Every sex trafficker of children is either knowingly or ignorantly deputized by the devil. This is why we all must be stilled and sobered when we think of his relentless, maniacal desires to consume this generation of infants and children.

Having now escaped the darkness that the enemy sought to suffocate me under as a child, I can see clearly multiple moments of strategy against my young life that were enacted by Satan and his demons. The first blow that I recognize has already been framed up in the first three chapters of this book as I detailed the impact of the implosion of my family. Now, I am going to share how the next volley of attacks came against me. This is the season when I actually began to cooperate with the enemy and the time of my life wherein I began to intentionally live far away from the Father.

In eighth grade, my neighborhood was rezoned by the county into a new school district. When my friends heard this, they were dismayed because they did not want to leave our current middle school in our last year and begin at the newly assigned school on the other side of Lilburn. I was actually excited about the change. Few kids knew me at Trickum Middle School where we were heading. I thought about this forthcoming big change all summer long. I determined to intentionally reinvent myself at my new school. I would no longer be the studious, humorous kid who played baseball and basketball. I determined that, on the first day of eighth grade, I would walk to the back seat of the bus where the tough, cool kids usually sat. I would wear a mean face. I would let my *aura* be that of the kid you did not want to mess with at school. I was still short, but I had begun lifting weights that summer and year three of puberty had given me a prematurely deep voice and man-jaw a good while before most of my friends. Basically, I determined to fake it so that I could make it. The wounding and anger that had been buried in my heart for nearly five years were beginning to sprout forth in my attitudes and actions. Smoke was beginning to plume out from that volcanic heart of mine. I decided that it was far easier for me to live in *proactive anger* than *reactive hurt*. Passively waiting for someone to rescue me from my inward fear had proven to be a failure. If nobody could comfort me, then I would take ownership of all my discomfort. In eighth and ninth grade, I fully gave myself over to the inner rage. I began to change, and the enemy of my soul provided every possible resource to help me along my way upon that path of destruction.

It was during this time that I forged a friendship with a handful of guys who were just as empty as I was. My best friends in the new school system ended up being Jeff and another friend that I will call Paul. Jeff's father had been murdered around the same time my mother had left me. It had left him reeling as a child. We were together a couple of orphan-spirited boys who became instant friends. Jeff was hilarious and we took pleasure in making one another laugh with our warped teenaged humor. Paul's unhappy heart was of the more traditional variety — broken home, indulgent 1980s parenting which allowed him nice clothes, a fast car, and regular access to cash. Paul was not as volatile as the two Jeffs, but we three quickly became inseparable. These two young men became my brothers. We really did become a family, albeit a highly dysfunctional one. It was deeply flawed love, but we loved each other the way a band of aimless brothers does. We went to lots of parties that summer, so we grew up in all the wrong ways at an accelerated rate. It was in a tent in Jeff's backyard that I got drunk and stoned for the very first time. I had been around alcohol and drugs before, but I never wanted to participate. That summer, my former desire to decline getting high went out the window, and it was not even a struggle when the newfound opportunity to become a teenage partier was presented to me. I had created a new family with Jeff and Paul, and now I had found a new identity: **I would be the kid who was the life of the party.** That would be the new me. I was surrounded by fellow fools and they made me their obnoxious Mayor!

My natural sense of humor was soon taken to an insane level under the influence of alcohol and drugs. More than once, one of my musical friends would sit at a piano in someone's house while his parents were out of town, and he would play while I would make up drunken, debauched songs of vice, singing at the top of my lungs among a multitude of wasted boys and girls who would give anything for a moment of laughter, however hollow it might be. During that summer after ninth grade, I learned how to expertly lie to my parents, stay gone from home for days at a time, roll a joint with one hand, make people laugh hysterically while dosing LSD, and cut lines of cocaine on a handheld mirror in the parking lot of Corinth Baptist Church in Mountain Park, Georgia.

Just typing that last sentence caused me to push back from my keyboard for a minute and ask, *"Really?"* The sad answer is, "Yes. Really." That is the description of the life I was choosing.

The enemy is skilled at the art of the setup. He found in me a willing participant. Though it likely sounds unbelievably awful to you as you read my summary of the summer of 1985, the truth is that it was actually a personal anesthesia from the pain inside of me. It is not rocket science, friends. People abuse alcohol and drugs to escape what they believe to be a greater threat, a deeper pain, a more frightening prospect that lives inside of them. Anything to escape the pain – that was the prize for which I began to live.

And thankfully, I believed, I did not have to do it alone anymore. We three dudes had each other. I had set out blindly to find myself a tribe.

I had succeeded.

CHAPTER 5
Stamping My Passport for the Far Country

"Not many days later, the younger son gathered all he had and took a journey into a far country, and there he squandered his property in reckless living."
– Luke 15:13

We Christians have a lot of room to grow in our communicating to others our testimony of being saved by the Father's amazing grace. Having now entered my third decade of local church ministry, I have listened to multiple people "share" in a gathering about how God rescued them from their sin. In some of these testimonial moments, we listeners had to hear *waaaaayyyy* too much information. When a salvation testimony is 80% focused on the details of a sordid past, and only 20% focused on exalting Jesus as the glorious, redeeming Savior, the witness has missed the mark. Sometimes, these well-intending but *filterless* witnesses in our churches produce little more than embarrassed, awkward silence from those listeners who wished that the testimony service had come with a gigantic mute button. As a new Christian, I went through a phase where my own personal testimony ended up talking too much about all the degradation and not enough of the deliverance. There later came a season where I started intentionally reading in the Bible how the Apostle Paul wrote about his own testimony. His pre-conversion life was abysmal. He was self-righteous, covetous, proud, blasphemous against Christ, pathologically religious, and an accomplice to unnumbered murders and false imprisonments against the early Jesus followers. What I began to take notice of was that Paul revealed his past transgressions with succinct headlines, almost never communicating all the salacious details. He saved the detailed version of his testimony for the communication of the components of God's beautiful transforming work of bringing him out of darkness and into the light. As a young believer, I decided that, whenever I shared my own story in the future, I should model my own approach after Paul's: **less of the degradation, more of the deliverance.**

Because of that insight about the best way to share one's story, I am going to make a conscious effort not to get bogged down in all of the nasty portions of my life between high school and my conversion to Christ at age twenty-four. I do not wish to feed that potential appetite in anyone who longs to know all of the juicy details of someone's formerly wicked ways. Frankly, those kinds of things are unprofitable. Out of respect for my beautiful, faithful wife and my precious kids, I am just going to summarize some aspects of those dark years with a summary headline that says, "Those lost days were comprised of all the types of behaviors that one might reasonably associate with the lifestyle of an unbridled alcoholic and drug user."

I was searching for belonging, purpose, and love. The more I failed to find those things, the more desperately I searched. The result was that I plunged further and further into a shameful, immoral abyss that left me far emptier than when I began.

Now, the details that *I will* provide you as you continue to read are important to the overall story of the Father's grace, mercy, and love to a wayward son who had wandered deeply into a far country, a great distance from Father's house. **I was still trying to figure it all out as I went.**

My parents were no fools. While they did not pry too deeply, they likely knew that I was not exactly an angel. Dad wanted me to excel in school and to cultivate a consistent work ethic. Somehow, in the midst of all of the partying, I managed to do both. I understood that, should I begin to fail my classes or experience any trouble with the law, Dad would drop the punitive hammer on me. Consequently, I became very shrewd, manipulating to my own advantage the systems that authorities placed over me. I learned to be respectful to all adults and to honor authority – at least outwardly. Paul's dad and Jeff's mom loved this about me because many of our other friends

25

were idiots at that time (sorry, guys). Some of our friends had already been caught in criminal behavior and thrown in jail. I worked hard to ensure that never happened to me or my buddies when I was with them. Additionally, I did well in school, with my lowest grade in high school being a singular C that I got in Physical Education one semester. Other than that, I made all A's and high B's. I got my first job in the fall of 1985 and worked twenty hours a week at a furniture store where I walked to work after school. I was never late for anything, I did my chores at home, completed my school assignments, and gave off the overall vibe of having it together. **Meanwhile, beneath the radar, I was rapidly becoming a teenage alcoholic.** I realized that, if I could check all the main boxes that dad required, I could erect an obscuring wall to all the eyes of authority, behind which wall I could enjoy all the forbidden activities that had become my true passions. This was that season in life wherein I became a crafty sinner. Deception is a skill, and it is actually possible for us to grow in the ability to use it. In the end, I became a proficient masquerader, fooling almost everyone almost all of the time. Only Paul and Jeff and some of our other friends knew what a mess I truly was. They did not mind. They were mostly messes too.

One defining moment that stands as a clear line that I crossed came in the spring of 1986. Jeff and I had become inseparable, but I still also had a connection to a Christian friend with whom I would occasionally hang out. One afternoon, Jeff and I were up to no good when this friend popped in. I cannot recall exactly how, but we talked my Christian friend into taking a half hit of LSD. Bowing to our peer pressure, he placed it on his tongue and hung out with us for about an hour. I remember him looking at his watch a little later and recognizing that he was going to be late for the Wednesday night youth group. He got up to head out the door and go to his church. For those of you who have never done drugs, you should know that LSD, also called *acid*, is an intense hallucinogenic. My Christian friend had never done *any* drug before that day, and now he was about to go to the house of God an hour after ingesting LSD. I had previously experimented with acid multiple times, so I knew what was coming his way, even though he had not yet begun to experience any effects of the drug making its way through his system. I had a full dose in me that day and was already starting to "trip" a little as my friend started to leave for the church. I could not let him go alone. *Friends don't let friends go to church on acid.* He stated that he felt fine and would not be talked out of going to youth group that night, so we two got in his car to leave.

I still cannot believe we did this. Our young lives were so empty and out of control.

Going to church on a Wednesday while under the influence of a hallucinogenic drug was not anything that I had ever envisioned for myself. I will spare you all the details, but suffice it to say, my friend's acid started impacting him about the same time we pulled into the church parking lot. Everything was warped and outside of the realm of reason. He began to look a little frazzled as the drug started distorting his sense of reality. Noting that he was not behaving like his usual self, other kids in the youth group were asking him if he felt okay. I could see that he was now getting hit hard by the drug and beginning to hallucinate. As we went inside the meeting room, he leaned over to me and whispered, "Are my arms on fire? Are those flames real?" It was in that moment that I grabbed him by his arm which, contrary to what he was seeing, was not actually engulfed in flames, and dragged him to the car in full sight of a room filled with about thirty teenagers. Though I was not a true Christian, I had enough good old cultural religion to terrify me that my rebellious pathway had lifted a defiant fist in the face of God that day. I chose to cause one of His true sons to momentarily go astray. I stepped into a house of worship under the influence of mind-altering drugs. Never before had I sensed that level of displeasure from God. I am not even saying for sure that God was actively enraged with me at that moment. My guess is that He was far more compassionate with me than I could have fathomed. I'm just saying that it felt like His wrath was hovering ten inches above my guilty head. On the ride home, I felt the deep accusation in my soul that I had crossed a line with the God in whom I had once believed. I really did consider myself — a Christian…in the Southern sense of the term. Now I had committed —

27

religious sacrilege of the highest degree, and I was confident that the Father was through with me. We somehow got home safely from church, and the next day, the drugs had left our system. We just went back to our normal suburban lives.

Among the scores of wrongdoings I committed in those far-country years, that particular event stands out to me as one wherein I slipped a long distance in the wrong direction, further away from the God who loved me. Satan, the accuser, used that event repeatedly to motivate me to run away from the God whom I believed certainly would never forgive such a thing. I began to "avoid God" at all costs, lest He catch me and crush me like Beanstalk Jack's angry giant.

Not surprisingly, my relationship with my Christian friend basically ended that day. He was so wise to get away from me. Many years later, I looked out from the pulpit where I was about to launch a Sunday morning message, and there he sat in the pew, smiling at me. He had heard that the troubled acid-tripping friend from his childhood had been radically saved by Jesus and was now a pastor of a local church. He came to see it all for himself. I am so glad that the Father gave him the opportunity to see His grace on my life. Personally, God also graced me to see my old friend that Sunday. He had pressed through that long-ago Wednesday-night failure, and he was able to stay in the Gospel stream that had saved him. God redeems and reconciles. He is a specialist at things like that.

By the way, that regrettable night in youth group in 1986 was the last time I set foot in a church until I was twenty-four years old. I had chosen to enter the out-of-control world of sin, vice, and wanton pleasure. God, in faithful pursuit, chose to bring me home to Himself many years later. *His grace is seemingly scandalous at times, isn't it?* He is so good to misguided masqueraders who travel along forbidden foot trails in the far country. Hallelujah, what a Savior.

CHAPTER 6
Exiting One Sewer, Entering Another

"Folly is a joy to him who lacks sense, but a man of understanding walks straight ahead."
- Proverbs 15:21

ABOUT AN HOUR AWAY FROM the home I now share with my family, and about a million miles away, is the house where I grew up in Lilburn. My kids groan whenever we are out that way and I choose to drive by that little place on Renee Court. It was a nice house forty years ago. Not so much anymore. What is crazy is that the same mailbox is still standing there from when I called that house my home. I remember my dad out there in the front yard with the post hole digger on the day he put it in the ground. The other thing that looks exactly the same is the drainage culvert at the top of our old driveway.

To keep rainwater from flowing down the incline of our driveway and flooding the yard, the original developer made sure to put a culvert with underground piping that carried the water past our house and dumped it into the creek behind the property line in our backyard. Atop the culvert was a removable cover that would allow a person to enter the drain and remove anything that might get washed down there and obstruct the water flow. Growing up, we always called it a sewer. Many times, we would have to remove the cover and climb down the five feet on the iron ladder to retrieve a baseball that had gotten away from us. I also remember that it was a great hiding place during long July days when we would play a large-scale game of hide-and-seek. One of the older boys once dared me to climb down there and crawl on my hands and knees through the entire length of the drainage pipe, all the way to the creek where it emptied. Wanting to impress, I rose to the challenge and did it. To my dismay, I found at about the midway point that there were all sorts of debris, garbage and even some decaying rodents scattered throughout the pipe. Having gone too far to turn back, I simply moved through all the disgusting contents of the pipe on my hands and knees and eventually rolled into the cool creek, feeling relieved that I had escaped with my life.

That journey through the so-called sewage pipe is a fitting metaphor of the time period that spanned my senior year at Parkview High School unto the day of my salvation in 1994. Those years were undoubtedly the worst of my life, and it is my relief to write about them here, and then roll out of the memory of them into the refreshing waters that awaited me in Jesus.

For me, by the end of this chapter, it is going to feel like exiting the sewer pipe. We are just about there. Breakthrough is coming. Light is soon to dawn. Hope is on the way. A King has mounted His steed and has determined a rescue. The ink is wet, and the good chapters will be written.

Just not quite yet.

My senior year at Parkview was unrestrained for me. I no longer cared about much. My friend, Jeff, had temporarily dropped out of school as his own internal struggles grew within him. Paul and I were now moving in a staggering two-legged race toward an undefined finish line. The parties were constant, not just on weekends. Our vices were still somehow manageable, but the ends were fraying quickly. Honestly, there were moments when I wondered if I would make it to graduation without first entering a jail cell or a body bag. Cocaine, meth, and other drugs were normal by the time I was a Junior at Parkview. We were smoking marijuana before school, after school, and sadly, during school. I recall coming home from school one afternoon and walking into my bedroom to find a large bag of weed, rolling papers, and my dope tray sitting on my desk in plain sight where I had left them out that morning before leaving for school. How had I escaped my parents walking by my open door and seeing it laying there in plain sight? My dad would have *freaked* had he seen my paraphernalia sitting there. For the record, drugs make you stupid. We thought back then that drugs enhanced our minds. **Wrong.** Drugs kill brain cells and shrink one's capacity to intellectually prosper. So foolish had I become, that I was leaving my drugs out in plain sight in my bedroom. In four years, I had gone from being intellectually sharp, quick-minded, and an acute thinker to becoming some kind of crossbreed between Elmer Fudd and Jeff Spicoli from *Fast Times at Ridgemont High*.

Perhaps most noteworthy is that I no longer cared about any loss, including loss of my formerly greatest strength: my mind. I had learned not to allow myself to feel anything anymore. I had become, as one of my favorite songs back then promoted, *comfortably numb*. Around this time, I also began hanging out with some adults who were making drugs and alcohol much more accessible to me. By age seventeen, I was both buying and selling drugs back and forth between people who were in their twenties, thirties, and forties. In those adults with whom I was partying, I was seeing a forecast of what my own life was going to look like when I got older. However, like most rebellious teenagers, I thought I was the invincible exception. I would never end up like these losers when I was in my thirties. I always assumed I would snap out of it. By this time, all of my closest friends had already been arrested at least once. I was the only one in my troubled tribe who made it all the way through high school having never been locked up, so I fancied myself a cut above all these others. I supposed that I was a higher caliber kind of miscreant. **The fact that I never got in trouble with the law in those teenage years was also God's grace.** Coursing within me was this death-wish recklessness coupled with an abject sadness that longed for all of my life's insanity to come to an end. I wasn't figuring out anything during this season in my languishing life.

My final year of high school was a fast-moving fog, and the time came to apply to colleges. Knowing exactly where I wanted to go to college, I only sent out one application. I got accepted to the University of Georgia on a track for a major in broadcasting. All my comedy and irreverent communication developed at parties and on long summer nights proved to align perfectly with the possibility of being a radio DJ, so that's the course

31

I charted. As graduation from Parkview came and went, it became time for my dad to cut a check to UGA for my initial round of tuition payments. Childhood was officially over and it was now time to begin to *adult* my way through the next chapter.

I started to panic.
Real life was finding me.
Suddenly, a collision between my awareness of how messed up I was slammed into a fear of the forthcoming disciplines that would need to accompany being a college student.

This weird thing called *adulthood* was on my heels. I was, by this time, clinically depressed, intermittently suicidal, chronically intoxicated and/or drugged, and about to be launched out of my parents' home to go and earn an education and pursue a career path. What incredible privilege had been afforded me, and I had squandered all of it. I was the stereotypical suburban kid who had a clear pathway to potential success cut out for him. My dad had never been one to just hand me money, but he gave me lots of opportunities to earn it. Now, he was ready to pay for a good college education and I was paralyzed in indecision, afraid to go. With just two months before classes were to begin, I asked my dad to talk with me. He did not really know how jacked up I was on the inside. I still possessed the skills to at least partially deceive my parents. They probably thought I drank a few beers on the weekends, but they could not have known the depths of my depravity and drug usage. I told dad that I didn't want to go to college. Surprised, he was not about to endorse that irresponsible decision. He reminded me that he had consistently told me over the years that I could live under his roof as long as I pursued an education. The conversation was not volatile, but dad was firm. He asked me to reconsider, but I declined my paid-for college education, and instead, I chose a slacker's path of going to find a job and go a little deeper into the quest to presumably figure it out as I go. Two days after that conversation with my dad about boycotting college, I moved out of my parents' home and into the townhouse of a husband and wife in their mid-twenties from whom I frequently bought drugs. I paid a hundred bucks a month to rent the room. As a teenager, I had previously worked part-time at a financial service company in the mailroom. I contacted some people who still worked there, and they pulled some strings to get me back on board with an entry-level job. Not uncharacteristically for me, I made a quick, firm decision to begin a new life chapter.

I left my father's house six weeks after my eighteenth birthday and never moved back. I was making $4.78 an hour as a clerk at my new job. I had finally exited the sewer of my painful childhood, *only to enter a different sewer of aimless adulthood.* Like I wrote earlier, drugs make people stupid, but that kind of life was, for me, more fun than being responsible, so I chose my lane and started to ride in it at full throttle.

Nobody could tell me what to do.

No parental parameters could suppress my unbridled enthusiasm for mischief anymore.

I would work my forty hours a week, sleep another forty hours and spend every other available moment pursuing whatever form of pleasure was closest at hand.

There was no plan – just impulsive reaction to whatever was in my face at the moment. It felt really good. At least, for a minute it felt good. Not too terribly long after, that kind of life would lose all the sense of pleasure, and the life I had chosen would turn into my own torment. The Father was on the throne for sure, but I had chosen to live my life running with the devil.

Before we move on, please note this little detail: that job at the financial services company which I took after leaving my parents' house was likely the peak decision of my own stupidity because, at that time, it replaced what might have been an eventual solid career in radio. **Yet, it was in that very office complex where I started working that, six years later, my**

33

life would intersect a servant of the Lord who made the spiritual needs of my utterly lost soul his two-year evangelistic bullseye. He would repeatedly try to hit that bullseye with Gospel truth arrows. God took my most foolish decision as a rebellious eighteen-year-old, and He sovereignly harnessed it as the beginning of a trajectory that would ultimately deposit me at the gateway to my eventual redemption. More about that a little later.

I did not know it at the time, but I was rolling out of the sewer and soon to experience the cleansing waters of grace.

CHAPTER 7

Guns, Groans, and the Grind

"You do not know what tomorrow will bring. What is your life?
For you are a mist that appears for a little time and then vanishes."
– James 4:14

LET ME SCOOT US AHEAD three years in time from the end of the last chapter. I was now twenty-one years old and living in a new apartment in a new city with my old friend, whom I am calling Paul. He was selling insurance, and I had moved up an inch or two on the food chain at the financial service company that employed me after I left my parents' home. At this time, some of the recklessness in my life had been curtailed just a bit. Drugs and alcohol were still my chosen gods, and I was well known in many of the local houses of whisky worship throughout Atlanta where, as one now of legal drinking age, I would saddle up to the bar and get my fill whenever I pleased. Paul and I had cultivated a new tribe of friends, and we had somewhat found a rhythm that provided us all an identity that orbited around a shared but unspoken sadness in our individual hearts. Because we were both making decent money, we could afford a nicer apartment where we regularly hosted parties. It was at one of those parties that a fairly dramatic wake-up call accosted me. Every story like this one needs one of those dramatic near-death moments. Well, I plan on supplying you with *two* before this book is finished. Here comes the first one.

On a chilly night, Paul invited a bunch of people over for a party. I remember not being too thrilled with his decision because I had to work the next morning. Even drunks have moments when the rigors of nonstop partying become a nuisance. Nonetheless, people started showing up and the normal sounds of Van Halen, Ozzy Osbourne, and Metallica began to seep through the stereo speakers. A few hours later, as things were thumping along pretty intensely, two guys showed up whom I did not recognize. They were clean-cut and stood out from the rest of us as we were a *wee-bit grungy* in our personal appearance. These two guys were rather drunk, and I remember feeling a little violated in my personal space as they both got louder inside my apartment. As one of the hosts, I casually asked them to step outside with me so I could find out who they were and how they ended up in my kitchen drinking my liquor. I have no memory of what was said, but things quickly turned heated, and a whole lot of back and forth erupted between me and one of the guys.

You know the old saying that teaches us that a person lives or dies by his or her words, right? **Well, I almost died by mine that night.** It turns out that these two clean-cut looking guys had recently returned from a tour of duty in Desert Storm, the first war America waged in Iraq. Obviously, one of them did not care much for a loud-mouthed, long-haired civilian who was cursing them out. Reaching his boiling point, he backed me up against the wall, pulled out a nickel-plated handgun with lightning speed and stuck it directly under my jaw. The whole thing lasted less than a minute, but I remember an awareness sweeping over me that I was about to exit planet earth. He was breathing heavy, leaning his face into my own with only the gun separating us. There were perhaps five seconds of silence after he asked me if I wanted to die right then and there. After that five seconds passed, I said to him, "Do it." I was not calling his bluff. I was truly expressing my desire to be done with life. Everyone around us thought that I was a courageous, no-fear wildman. The reality was that I was still an open-wound fourth grader who was tired of trying to make it another day. I embraced death at that moment and looked that dude right in the eye, waiting *for the dark to swallow me.* I remember a flicker of a thought that wondered if I would hear the gunshot when it came.

It turned out that he had no intention to kill me. He let me go, put the gun in his waistband, and extended his hand to shake mine. Somehow, he earned some distorted form of respect for me at that moment. We walked back inside the apartment, laughed it off, and saddled back up to the kitchen bar. The party went on and I dismissed the near-death moment as I poured another drink. I do not remember that gun-toting fellow's name, but I will never forget his face. *His was almost the last face I ever saw in this life.* The next morning, a frightening clarity began to come to me in strong waves of internal groans and questioning:

> *Jeff, what are you doing?*
> *Look at your life – is this really you?*
> *Did you consider that you would have gone straight to Hell last night if you had died?*
> *How much farther down this road do you plan to go?*

As with all other days during that season in my life, there were only questions. No answers. I still was not figuring out anything of importance. When the Gospel came to me three years later, the answers finally began to come also, but not that day. Only emptiness and one more degree of dropping deeper down into the place of hopelessness. Sitting here right now, I am again sobered that, if that soldier had pulled the trigger, I would still be in the place of forever judgment right now. That is the reality. I would have died that night in my sins and entered the everlasting abode of the unforgiven. You would think that this near-death event would have been sufficient to shake me into humility. Not even close. I just went right back into autopilot and picked up where I left off. I resumed the grind of life, assuming I could keep on attempting to figure it out as I went.

Any reasonable observer could have seen that I was not figuring out a thing. This was when God seemed to take a much more intense initiative with me. It was like the Father of this prodigal son took off running toward the defeated and dirty boy who still could not quite find his way home.

This immeasurably, merciful Father, whom I had continually rejected and refused, decided it was the right time to speak stoutly into my sad life, so He dispatched a human voice to me, crying out into my wilderness with truth and invitation. He was going to bring me home.

CHAPTER 8

God Dispatches a Prophet

"There was a man sent from God, whose name was..."
– John 1:6

SCOTT. HIS NAME WAS SCOTT. I found that out later. I had seen him for about a year prior, moving around the hallways of the place where we both worked. He looked about my age – early twenties. There was something *on him* that gave off of him a vibe of him having it together. He moved with purpose and carried an intensity, the source of which was difficult for me to pinpoint. I was a bit of a punk and didn't find myself thrilled with the prospect of another young dude, taller than me, better looking than me, moving throughout the workplace where I had established myself as the cool, young guy. I was still desperate for identity back then, and this new dude might be a threat to the territory I had carved out for myself at work. We were in different departments, but I would bump into Scott from time to time as we passed in the halls. I do not think we ever spoke more than a cursory, "Hey. What's up?" One day, I stopped seeing him walking the halls. He vanished. My guess was that he quit and found a better job, as the company had much employee turnover. A few months later, I learned that there was a nightshift opening in a different department. The work schedule for the position was three days on, four days off every week. That really appealed to me because it would open a door of four days of partying for me every week. When I found out that there was a ten percent pay upgrade due to it being on the nightshift, I applied for the position. A week later, the transfer was approved, and I was given my orders to report to begin my new work at the company.

When I showed up that first night, my manager took me back to our work area and introduced me to the team on which I had been placed. Surprisingly, there was that young guy that I assumed had left the company. He introduced himself to me with a smile and a handshake. That is when

I learned that his name was Scott. He would be training me one-on-one. I played it cool, not giving any hint that I was not really thrilled to be working alongside the competition. Scott was friendly and also a good trainer. In the first hour of my learning from him, he broached the subject of faith, God, and Christianity. Mind you, back then our culture was not as hair-trigger sensitive as it is now. Political correctness had not been enthroned in Atlanta. I was not offended in the least by his injection of his Christian faith into our conversation because I also considered myself a Christian. I told Scott that I had asked Jesus into my heart and had later been baptized as a young person, and that I believed Jesus to be the Son of God and Savior. All those church-going years as a child had not been a complete waste. I knew all of the necessary lingo. What I was not prepared for was Scott's over-the-top reaction to my declaration of being a believer in Jesus. He somewhat experienced a joy explosion, calling me *brother* and saying a bunch of Amen-Hallelujah-Ain't-God-Good kind of stuff. I imagine his enthusiasm was quickly curbed when I stared back at him like he had something hanging out of his nose. I remember telling him, "Dude, I'm not *that kind* of Christian."

A few years later, Scott would tell me that he felt God gave him an assignment at that very moment. He was going to conquer this rebel named Jeff with the Gospel of Jesus' grace and love. For the next two-plus years, God saw to it that I would spend no fewer than twenty hours a week joined at the hip with Scott as we worked. **By the way, did I mention that Scott was a bi-vocational Southern Baptist youth pastor whose deepest passion was to engage in a lifestyle of confrontational evangelism?** His real calling was at his church, while his paying job was right there where I was also working. Do not tell me that God is not sovereign, friends! He put the rebel right next to the Reverend for forty hours a week! Here I was: a defeated, depressed, addicted and borderline-insane young man drowning in his sins. What did God do? He vocationally chains me to a fiery Baptist evangelist, slathered in zeal for lost souls and frothing at the mouth to see Jeff Lyle bow his heart to King Jesus.

I didn't stand a chance.

Over the next two years, Scott would move intentionally between verbally witnessing to me (yes, at work), placing Gospel pamphlets in my lunch bag in the break room refrigerator, recapping his pastor's sermons from Sunday to me, and taking me to dinner where he would play nonstop Christian music in his car on the way. Scott was relentlessly determined to win me to his King. He did not pretend to approve of my lifestyle as he came to know over time what I was all about, but he genuinely cared for my soul. He was firm in his challenges to me about my enjoyment of my sin, but I never felt condemned by Scott. Over time, I found myself hungering for whatever it was that Scott had, which I knew that I did not have. One night, he asked me to come to his car on our break. He did not know it, but I was heavily using cocaine at that time. **That drug has a special touch of Satan on it**, and my growing usage of it left me in a level of depression that regularly had me considering suicide. That particular night, I was in a very dark place and extremely tender of heart and vulnerable in my spirit. All these years later, I wonder if the Holy Spirit clued Scott in to my potential to be receptive to the Gospel that night. I agreed to sit in his car with him as we ate a snack and drank a soda. Scott lovingly and quickly ambushed me with a Gospel song on a cassette tape that had me weeping in less than a minute. When the song ended, he calmly shared again with me my deep need for Jesus. Scott's biggest obstacle was figuring out how to topple the religious, culturally-Christianized monument erected in my heart to which I was holding. Like many church kids, I had prayed the sinner's prayer, and I believed that long-ago prayer to be my ticket to Heaven. I was too proud (frightened?) to admit that the prayer from my childhood was meaningless and impotent. I was literally living like a future inhabitant of Hell while presuming to be a citizen of Heaven. Scott was going so strongly after my heart that night, and I was so close to humbling myself and admitting that I was no Christian in the biblical sense. He had been promoted to my boss by this time, and we had gone well over our twenty minutes of allocated break time. I knew if I could resist his witness to me for just a little longer, we would have to go back inside since he was the boss. He pressed a little harder, but I ratcheted up my resolve, looked up at him through streaming tears and lied through my teeth, "I'm fine, Scott. Leave me alone about this, please."

Thank God that he never considered honoring my request to be fully left alone. That night was in the late autumn of 1993.

At the beginning of 1994, just a handful of months before I came to Christ, God set up the last circumstantial piece of the puzzle that would ultimately lead to my deliverance. I was moved into a position that placed me side by side with Scott for thirteen hours a day at work. Thirteen hours a day is not a short time to sit next to an evangelistic Baptist who has made it his aim to win you into the Kingdom! By the way, I thank God for the Baptists. No other denomination has remained fully committed to training in personal evangelism more so than the Baptists. Scott was not, however, representing a denomination to me. He was an ambassador for Jesus, and the man was relentless.

During those work hours, he and I would monitor computer screens which would periodically alert us to a series of tasks that would need to be completed. Between those alerts, there would sometimes be three or four hours where there was literally nothing for us to do. I am confident that the company has long since streamlined their processes for better productivity, but in those days, there was plenty of "hurry up and wait." Why is this detail important? Because during those dead hours, we were permitted to read books, as long as we did not vacate the desk where the monitors sat. Scott, of course, read his Bible. Every day. All day. *Sometimes out loud.* He would frequently ask me to quiz him on Bible verses that he was trying to memorize. He would have multiple pages of Scripture written out in his own handwriting, and he would ask me to read them as he recited them, ensuring that he was saying them back perfectly to me. *He was a slick little sucker.* He knew what he was doing. My reading those verses as he recited them opened up conversations about God, sin, true salvation, grace, and righteousness. He had set me up and it was working. One day, as we migrated through Galatians chapter five, Scott had me read aloud the differences highlighted in those verses between the fruit of the Holy Spirit and the sinful works of the flesh. I had none of the fruit of the Spirit in my life, and I was convincingly guilty of most of the works of the flesh.

41

I remember him asking me to read the end of Galatians 5:21 out loud multiple times. Concerning those people who live for the passions of their flesh, that verse declares, "I warn you, as I warned you before, that **those who do such things will not inherit the Kingdom of God**."

When I read those words, it felt like a bolt of lightning spiked down from Heaven into my soul. There it was. I could not deny it. The very things that my life had been characterized by for the previous ten years were the clear context for the warning of Galatians 5:21. No matter what I felt, what I hoped, or what I blindly clung to, the Bible declared that I, and people like me, could not, as we were, inherit the Kingdom of God. **Simply put, nobody whose life is predominated by sinful works of the flesh has any legitimate claim to being born again.** It does not matter how many times they prayed the sinner's prayer, how often they might have been baptized, or what church had their names on a membership roll. That verse taught me that day the truth that **a** faith that ultimately saves will undoubtedly behave.

My sins had found me out. I was sober that day and had no barriers to prevent God's truth from penetrating my darkened heart. Interestingly, I do not remember feeling terrified. I felt sadness. It was as if the last thing that I clung to in order to help me feel safe had now been removed. For the very first time in my life, I found myself standing naked and exposed before God.

I did not know what to do.

Scott must have seen a change in my countenance. He asked me what that verse in Galatians was saying to me. After two years of faithful, relentless witnessing about Jesus to me, Scott heard from my lips the words he had longed to hear when I mumbled to him, "Uhmmm…I guess I am not saved. These verses say I am not truly a Christian."

With great maturity and patience, he let the moment hang in the air for a bit. He calmly and kindly told me that he was glad that I rightly understood what the Bible was saying there. He did not press me for a decision. He must have known this was a breakthrough moment in God's work in my life. He became quiet, and a few moments later, the computer monitors signaled a new run of tasks that we needed to complete. His human voice went silent for the rest of the day, but Heaven's witness did not cease His communication. God the Spirit kept right on speaking to me.

Somewhere in the early spring of 1994, I understood the reality that I was not a true Christian. What I had believed in my mind about Jesus had never actually made it into my heart. My intellect had been convinced for years concerning the Gospel, but I had never surrendered to the Father in my personal will. Sure, I had prayed a naïve, religious prayer as a child to welcome Jesus in my heart, but I had never repented of my sin. Consequently, Jesus had never entered my life. I knew it for sure at that moment, but the enemy would redouble his efforts to reestablish that misplaced confidence in that *Jesus-come-into-my-heart* prayer I had offered as a child. At that moment, though, all illusion was removed. I saw myself as a spiritually lost sinner. It was a devastating blow to the charade that had become my life.

Jesus, through a man named Scott, had pierced into my illusion. Just a few months later, the victory came in fullness.

CHAPTER 9

My Last Week as a Lost Man

"I am severely afflicted; give me life, O LORD, according to Your word!"
- Psalm 119:107

SCOTT HAD LEFT ME IN a place that I did not want to go. After that intense revelation from the book of Galatians about my counterfeit Christianity, I intentionally began to pull away from Scott. Whether he sensed it or not, I noticed that he also seemed to be pulling back. Likely aware that I had experienced the heights of conviction about my need for repentance, Scott must have been discouraged when I did not follow up with a commitment of myself to Christ in the days which followed. Honestly, there was little more that he could possibly do for my soul. I did not need yet another sermon, another song, or an additional Gospel tract in my lunch bag. **He knew that it was now up to me.** For a couple of years, he had invited me to come to his church. I always backed out at the last minute. I always assumed that there would be another invitation from him and that I would eventually go. He let me know one day that they had promoted him within the department and had moved him to the day shift. Our sequestered times together on night shift were coming to an end in a few days. When he began his new role and was no longer by my side four days each week, I realized that I had been living vicariously through Scott's faith. I had been *spiritually drafting* behind him. My attachment to him had felt to me like a lifeline to God. As long as Scott was around, I felt like I could get from God whatever I needed whenever I wanted. Now, the only Christian in my life was gone and I was on my own.

In my private life, the addictions had reached new heights. You know that you are in really bad shape when your drunk friends and fellow addicts are counseling you to get help with your life. I had already spent a week in a detox center which yielded zero results. It got to the point where I was staying in my apartment by myself on weekends and using cocaine alone. A demonic paranoia began to own me through the use of that particular drug. Some of you will choke on what I am about to say, but I promise it is absolutely true. One night, after getting into bed half drunk, I awoke a few hours later to a paralyzing sense of dread filling the room. I could not move my body, but I opened my eyes and saw two *things* at the foot of my bed. I was not dreaming in my sleep or hallucinating in my awakened state. Whatever the two things were, they were not human…*and they were not good.*

One was short and one was taller, and they stood there as I stared at them in growing terror. I was seized with a dread that I had never felt before, even though I had been in seances and lots of New Age occultic activities over the years. I had spent a weekend less than a year before with some practicing Satanists as they sought to recruit me to come to one of their meetings in a field. Those moments were intense too, but this unfolding scene in my bedroom was in a category all its own. The only detail I can clearly recall was that the shorter of the two things watching me had a face similar to that of a toad. The degree of ugliness on both of them was otherworldly. It felt to me that they were present in the room to do something to me. I could not move. I was functionally paralyzed and filled with the deepest fear I had ever experienced. My eyes were open but even my face muscles were frozen. In desperation, I cried out through unmoving lips and over my paralyzed tongue, "Jesus. Jesus. JESUS!" I remember watching the two things begin to fade away when I spoke the name of the Lord – almost like a slow dissolve transition used by those who edit video. They seemed to be leaving the room. Within a few seconds, they were totally gone from my sight. My ability to move returned, and I rolled over on my side and cried myself back to sleep. Being 100% ignorant of any theology of demons, angels, or spiritual warfare, I still had no uncertainty about where the two things had come from. For those of you who may think it was just an effect of drugs in my system, I assure you it was not. After ten years of abusing all sorts of drugs, I knew when I was hallucinating and when I was not. The sense of evil in the room is what woke me up, not the appearance of these two things. It was only after the sense of dread awakened me that I saw them with my physical

45

eyes. In my apartment that night, I had experienced the visible presence of two demons who possessed full and open access to my life. My guess is that they had been trailing me for a very long time, but that night *I saw them*.

Things were getting very intense for me in those days right before my conversion. I was lingering at a crossroads with zero wisdom to know which way to go.

What I believe was occurring in my life during those last months and weeks before my salvation was nothing short of a final assault by Satan to destroy me. The enemy has observed human nature since the Garden of Eden. While Satan and his demons are not all-knowing, *they are observant*. They can recognize when the Father is working to bring lost sinners to Himself. **Remember, every lost sinner belongs to Satan. He is their father until they are born again and brought into the family of God through repentance and faith in the sacrifice of Jesus Christ.** Satan's strategy had been very successful in my life for twenty-four years. I was going to be one of his *slow kills*. As he observed the hand of God strongly moving on my behalf to redeem me in 1994, I am convinced that he heightened his attempts to destroy me. The demonic visitation in my bedroom was immediately followed up with an unprecedented open door to sin and vice during the spring and early summer of that year. I remember people literally giving me free drugs, primarily cocaine and ecstasy. Every bar I went to had people ready and eager to pick up my tab for drinks. I drove drunk constantly and should have died in a mangled twisting of metal. Looking back, it was as if the enemy was seeking to poison me unto the point of overdose. The lowest, most humiliating moment of my drug usage also occurred during this time. The enemy was using my willing commitment to drug abuse to rob me of my sanity.

Alone in my apartment on a particular weekday, I began using cocaine early in the morning. By lunchtime, I was pretty much out of my mind and being hounded by intense paranoia. I found myself looking out the peephole of the front door in order to get a head start on anyone who might be

46

hiding out there, *trying to undo me.* I literally spent three or four consecutive hours at that peephole that day. Each time I put my eye on the little lens, I believed I saw a giant, multicolored parrot walking back and forth on the steps that were just outside the door. I knew I was hallucinating, but I couldn't suppress the cocaine-fueled compulsion to try to catch the mutant parrot. I absurdly felt that it was spying on me. I would yank the door open to run out and catch it, but of course, it was not there. I remember arguing with myself out loud that I was simply hallucinating and to stop looking out the peephole for the nonexistent bird. This happened over and over for hours. It was on this day that I knew that the drugs were going to take me into a level of mental illness from which I would not likely return. Somehow, I determined as the sun went down that day, I would walk away from cocaine for good. I was terribly frightened by how low I had sunk. For whatever reason, that particular drug seemed to open up a portal to spiritual darkness that, even in my lostness, I wanted nothing more to do with. God had mercy on me, and I never used cocaine again after I finished what I had in a little baggie that night. That is not to say that I got completely clean of drugs – not even close. I continued to smoke marijuana as often as I could and took doses of ecstasy on the weekends. **I was still a slave.** Though I was denying myself further use of cocaine, I had merely exchanged one set of shackles for another as my use of ecstasy increased significantly. I was so utterly lost, and humanly speaking, there simply was no conceivable way out.

There was nothing to figure out at this point. I had quit trying because I no longer believed in anything. *There would be no rescue. There was no hope. Love was a myth and truth an illusion. God existed but I had rebelled against Him for so long that I just knew for a fact that He would never receive me.* At this point, there was nothing left to try and figure out because there was nothing that really mattered.

All I truly believed was that there was nothing left in which to believe.

This is a perfect opportunity for me to insert a few Kingdom truths about God. As you have continued to press on with me in my story, I commend you. *It is depressing. It is shameful.* Some of you who are reading had no clue concerning the depths of darkness in which I once daily lived.

Do you know why you had no clue before reading what I have written?

Because God's grace and redemption are immeasurably more potent than human sin and enslavement.

By His mercy, I have now lived longer in His deliverance than I did in my former degradation. I have been revealing thus far in my story the *before version* of me. You likely have only known of the *after version* of me. I have been describing the ruin of my life when you have only known the redemption of my life. I want to take just a moment here and declare without reservation that the only reason why I am now living a victorious, blessed, and meaningful life is because of the Lord Jesus Christ. **It's Him. It's Jesus.** I did not actually quit drugs – I was supernaturally delivered by the power of the Son of God from the chains of addiction. I did not become resolved or moral – I was resurrected and radically transformed by the power of the Spirit of God. I did not exit a destructive phase of life – I was chosen before the foundation of the world by God the Father who brought me into His family through repentance and faith in His only begotten Son. I have only included a tiny fraction of detail concerning my miserable life as a lost man. I wanted to reveal just enough for you to have the awareness of the astounding powers of transformation that are inherent in the Gospel of Jesus Christ. **Everything I am now I owe to Him.** He did not do half and ask me to accomplish the other half. We did not team up for my deliverance. I want to be abundantly clear: the pre-conversion version of Jeff Lyle was a dead man walking. I was a bad human being. I was wicked to the core. The evidence of why God's grace is so scandalous is seen in His determined pursuit of me – not to destroy me, but to save me and demonstrate His love for me. He made me the unmissable bullseye for His redeeming love.

Yes, the Father loved me in my lostness. He had compassion on me in my pain. He poured out a waterfall of mercy upon me in my rebellion like the roaring waters of Niagara Falls being funneled down to land upon a singular acorn. He could have destroyed me and been worthy of eons of praise by Heaven's angels for doing so. Instead of pouring His wrath upon me, the Father poured it upon His Son, Jesus, on the cross. Jesus took my punishment upon Himself. The judgment for my sin (and your own) was placed upon Him as God's sacrificial lamb. Because of that transaction, lavish mercy found my sin-sickened soul. For years, I had lifted a hand of defiance to God. In the end, He extended a hand of grace to me. This is the essence of what it means to be saved, to be born again through faith in Jesus Christ. Jesus gets all of my bad. I get all of Jesus' good. Forgiveness is all by the grace of God to anyone who will believe and repent, turning from ruling their lives to bowing before the King of the ages. Jesus will save anyone. *Anyone.*

There may very well be someone in your life who seems as lost as I once was. **Don't you dare give up on them.** Their addictions are no match for the restorative power of the Holy Spirit. That person's demons can be scattered and crushed by a single whisper of protection from Heaven's throne room. It does not require any evidence of possibility beforehand to ensure that a person can be saved. Whether it be the thief on the cross, hours before his death, Saul of Tarsus on his way to Damascus to kill some more Christians, or a twenty-four-year-old addict in Bible-belt-Georgia… God requires no assistance to bring the miracle of salvation to those whom He has loved. Please remember the potency of that truth as you consider all the seemingly hopeless people that you come across in life. They are the beloved of God. **They are worthy of all of us who are Jesus-followers never giving up on them.** God is able, and you and I simply cannot know when their breaking point will arrive. When it does, if they will look to Him, His mercy will be there to catch them.

Now, let me take you to my final week as a lost man. At this point in reading, you should picture yourself as someone who has been in a really deep and dark cave but is now approaching the opening of that cave where light is pouring in. We are about to get free together as we exit the exhausting narrative of my sin, my sadness, and Satan's unraveling plot against me. Here comes King Jesus! The enemy is about to taste defeat again. Bear with me just a little longer so we can knock out the last little trickling details of the first few days of August in 1994.

Every now and then, a change in schedule would hit the night shift in my department at work. The result was that, on that transition week which occurred twice a year, I would get eight paid days off in a row. It was a true perk of working in that department. As summer was drawing to an end, my eight days of freedom arrived. I had met some people at a local bar a few days earlier, and we had spontaneously decided to ride as a group down to Panama City, Florida. All of my previously close-knit tribe had grown a little weary of me in those last days. My former friends simply had gotten sick of the depression, paranoia, and volatility that kept surfacing in my life. *The guy who was once the life of the party had become the death of it.* Nobody wants to hang out with a guy who bird-watches through a peephole and chases imaginary parrots as his hobby. This new group of friends I had just met did not know me well, so they were happy to head down to the beach with me. Frankly, nearly everything about those days at the beach has gone completely dark in my memory. What follows is what I remember that needs to be shared. When I wrote that this book would contain two separate near-death encounters for me, I reserved the second one for now. It signaled what I now am convinced was my last chance to repent and turn my life over to Jesus. I cannot prove that, but I believe it with all my heart.

Somebody gave me a free ecstasy pill on August 2nd, 1994. Already drunk, I took the pill without hesitation. What I could not have known was that this particular pill came from a botched batch. Whoever created that batch of MDMA got the ingredients wrong in some unknown way. The result was that several people in Panama City were experiencing some undesirable effects from the ecstasy being passed around that week. I would be one of them. Shortly after taking the drug, I began to experience a level of hallucination that is not typically associated with MDMA or, by its street name, *ecstasy*. Quickly, my body temperature began to spike intensely on the already scorching-hot balcony of the beach condo we were renting. I recall that all the voices and sounds around me began to have a heavy reverb to it that made me want to pull my ears off. It was like an endless cycle of repeated echoes, but it was on the inside of my head. My last conscious memory was of some guy named Randy, who could clearly see that I was struggling, forcing me to sit in a chair while he and his girlfriend kept pouring buckets of ice-cold water over my head to help drop my body temperature. I remember some dreadful moments wherein I felt physical life draining out of me. I was consciously afraid, but I was physically unable to do anything but sit there in that chair and wait on death to come. For the first time after a decade of drug abuse, I was experiencing an overdose. Somewhere during their attempts to help me, I blacked out completely in the presence of my new friends and found out later from them that I had convulsed on and off in that balcony chair for close to an hour. When I awoke, I was still sitting in the same chair, and the sun was setting on the horizon where the sky and ocean kissed each other. The lighter side of the drug was still impacting me, but it was in a more pleasing way that is consistent with the reasons that most people take ecstasy.

I had somehow survived. *Again.*

I knew that I had never come as close to death as I had at that moment. The whole experience was so subjective and impossible to define, but I have always felt that I went *elsewhere* during that balcony blackout. When I sobered up in the days that followed, I could not shake the sense that my time of defying God and getting away with it was over. The next morning, we made the long drive home to Georgia. The whole way home, I never spoke. I understood that I had nearly died again. In about thirty-six hours, I was due back at work, and the enormity of what had happened at the beach began to weigh me down emotionally. I so wish that I could have a record of what all was racing through my mind and heart on the way home from Florida. I know that there was the consideration of suicide again when I got home. Another stint in rehab also seemed like something I might possibly explore. I really wanted help, but at this point in my life, there was no longer such a thing as hope in me. I recognized that what would likely happen is that I would go home and sleep, get up and go to work the next night, and resume my ingrained patterns of alcoholism and drug abuse. That's what I now clearly was: a drunken, drug-abusing loser who would never change.

I showed up at work at 7:00 p.m. on the night of August 3rd. It was an uneventful night and it concluded with a very slow workflow in the morning hours as I prepared to go home. That morning, I was leaving work when my old friend, Scott, was entering the building to begin the day shift in the data center. I was so glad to see him. His was the only face of hope in my life. Desperate to reconnect a little with him, I initiated small talk and then I told him for the hundredth time that I wanted to go to church with him that Sunday. Ever the voice of God in my life during that season, I will never forget the words that came out of Scott's mouth as he firmly placed his Bible on the counter at the security desk. He looked me squarely in the eyes, almost glaring at me, and said,

> **"You don't need to go to church, Jeff. You need to go home right now, fall on your face and surrender to Jesus Christ as the Lord over your life."**

With that, he picked his Bible back up, kept looking me in the eye and then turned away to walk down the hallway without saying another word.

Gripped, I exited the building, opened the door of my truck with my keys in a trembling hand, and drove the half mile back to my apartment. Scott had spoken those words to me, but God was the One doing all the subsequent communication. I had no vocabulary for what I felt at that moment, but now I know that the fear of the Lord was resting on me. My little Isuzu low-rider truck was filled with the presence of God as I made my way home. It was NOT pleasant. It was overwhelmingly intense, and it was owning me, reducing me, bringing me to a place of self-renunciation. I pulled into the apartment complex on Sweetwater Road. My head was swimming as I approached Apartment Number 112 and somehow steadied my still shaking hand to get the key in the door. The apartment was empty as I walked in, and I deadbolted the door behind me. The weight of God's presence was getting heavier and heavier upon me. I entered the first room on the left in the hallway, my bedroom. I closed my door and fell down under the weight of God's presence next to the mattress on the floor that served as my bed. My soul exploded right then and there as I felt glued to the floor in a torrent of emotions.

I was weeping uncontrollably. It was a feeling I had never experienced before, and it was increasing in intensity by the second.

Heaving, sobbing, I was choking on twenty-four years of pain and shame that were being extracted from my soul. I could not muffle my cries. It would have sounded like a wounded animal to anyone who was listening.

The only words I could form were soon to come out of my mouth. Those words would frame up the most pathetic-sounding prayer I have ever offered to God. Those words were the very ones that the Lord had waited to hear from me. Those words were the most raw and honest things that had ever come from my mouth.

Everything, and I mean *everything*, was about to change.

It was about 9:00 a.m.

It was August 4th, 1994.

SECTION 3
UNTO HIM

CHAPTER 10
My Own Personal Easter

"There is therefore now no condemnation for those who are in Christ Jesus.
For the law of the Spirit of life has set you free in Christ Jesus
from the law of sin and death."
- Romans 8:1-2

My wife, Amy, is not a big fan of surprises. A few years after we were married, I thought it would be a marvelous idea to throw her a surprise party at her Aunt Darlene's house. Working covertly, I was so proud of myself as I networked with family and a few of Amy's girlfriends to ambush my sweetie pie with a decently sized surprise birthday party. I had asked her earlier that week to block out that particular night so that I could take her to a romantic dinner *with just us*. I strategized to tell her that we could drop off our daughter, Alicia, at her aunt's home so that they could watch her while we enjoyed our little rendezvous at a nearby restaurant. Amy got ready and I remember having a little twinge of *uh-oh* when she came out of our bedroom looking really fine. Makeup, hair, and a really good-looking outfit were only *out-beautified* by the excited smile on her face. We had not gotten a lot of time together during that season so, as I found out later, she was really looking forward to our time together. Well, forty minutes later when we got to her aunt's home and entered, the twenty voices crying out, "Surprise!!!" caused all the blood to rush up into her pretty face as an admixture of embarrassment and disappointment hit her. She instantly realized that this would not be a romantic night for us as a couple. It was a party – and my introverted wife was completely ambushed. The Bible actually teaches in 1ˢᵗ Peter 3:7 that husbands must live knowledgeably with their wives. I was supposed to know her well enough to discern that the last thing Amy would have wanted to do on her birthday was to spend it in a room full of people. That was a very long time ago. It was also the last time I surprised my wife with a party. Note to self: not everyone enjoys surprises…especially Amy Lyle on her birthday. *Live and learn, fellas.* I was figuring things out as I go.

Speaking of big surprises, let me resume my recounting of the morning of August 4th, 1994. As the presence of God was filling my little bedroom, I was about to experience the most surprising thing that had ever occurred in my life up to that point. God sent me no notice ahead of time. The angel, Gabriel, did not descend to forecast what was about to happen to me. There was no announcement, *only arrival.* The weight of my sin inside of me was met by the weight of God's presence all around me. I had fallen to my knees next to my bed. For some reason, as I knelt there with my face close to the floor, I recall seeing through my tears that the little patch of carpet under my face was really gross. While all of Heaven was beginning to break loose, my mind was processing the several different shades of gray and brown that colored the matted carpet in front of me. I remember that it smelled like beer. It was a fitting metaphor because that grungy, matted, and beer-soaked carpet was emblematic of the condition of my soul. I could almost hear the Holy Spirit saying to me, "Say goodbye to the old life, Jeff. I am about to remove it. Here comes the new."

While still sobbing uncontrollably, I knew I needed to communicate something to God. I did not know the proper way to announce a surrender because I had always lived as a stubborn fighter. There was no Scott in the room with me; no priest, no pastor, no counselor was present. There was just God and me. I remember almost to the letter the words I released. Rocking back on my knees and looking up toward Heaven, I groaned the following words:

"**God, I have ruined my life. That preacher at work told me that You would save me if I called out to You. I do not care if You save me or if you kill me, but I am done running from You. Here is my life. I've ruined it. It is Yours. Take it.**"

58

That was it.

I did not even say *"amen"* or *"in Jesus name"*, or anything else that would have sounded remotely pious. That prayer was nothing but a soul grunt from a man who had finally brought out his white flag. It was a pathetic surrender; spoken in a level of weakness that I had never embraced up to that point in life. Yet, those were the most powerful words that had ever come out of my mouth. I did not understand what had occurred right then, but God would remove all doubt some time later.

After I finished verbally forming my surrender, I literally rolled from the place I was kneeling and onto the mattress laying on the floor. I pulled the sheet over my body and fell immediately asleep. When I awoke about eight hours later to get ready for another night at work, I sensed something different. It wasn't anything in particular that was different, just an *undefined difference* all around me. By God's grace, there were no drugs or alcohol in the house to tempt me out of habit to do what I had done nearly every year for a decade. As a matter of fact, the two days prior were the first back-to-back days in months where I had not ingested alcohol or drugs. I drove to work and began another thirteen-hour shift. Now, mind you, I did not believe that I had been "saved" earlier that morning. I simply thought I had surrendered my life to Jesus at a full and final level. Funny, that actually defines what salvation is – **a full surrender to Jesus Christ as Lord** – but I was still clinging to that repeating of the sinner's prayer in my childhood as my personal salvation moment. In my biblically ignorant opinion, this thing that happened on the floor of my apartment about ten hours before was something different than being saved. What had happened to me must have been beyond salvation. It must have been, I reasoned, something *extra*.

Right before my shift ended, I felt like I needed to tell Scott that I had done what he had told me to do the morning before. I logged on to the interdepartmental messaging system and sent him a note. I wrote to him that I had surrendered my life to Jesus. Before sending the note, I paused and then added**, "I am now a brand-new man."** Shortly after sending the email, I headed home and got the second session of deep, peaceful sleep in two days. I remember looking around at the streets and lawns as I drove the short distance back to the apartment that morning. It was very strange, but the sky appeared to be a shade of blue like I had never seen. It sounds cliché, but the grass really did look greener, and the landscaped entrance to my apartment complex popped in a polychromatic vibrancy that made me feel like I was driving past a hi-definition portal into the Garden of Eden. Maybe it was just because I had been sober for a couple of days, but I felt like I had new eyes or something. There was a cool breeze which struck me as strange because it was early August in Georgia. The asphalt should have been melting, but the air as I exited my truck was clean and refreshing. *Weird.* I walked in the apartment and said good morning to my roommate of just a few months, who was heading out to install carpet for the day. Then I laid down in bed. Many months before, Scott had given me a big, blue hard-backed study Bible. I saw it on an end table, the only piece of furniture in my room. I picked it up and laid down in bed to read a little in it. This Bible had all sorts of notes in it. For some reason, I flipped it open to a place called Philippians. After finishing all four chapters, I felt like I had gobbled down some spiritual vitamins. **Something stirred deeply in me as I read my Bible.** Looking back, I think I was experiencing the movement of the Holy Spirit within my newly cleansed human spirit. I simply had no grid to define the strangely pleasant sensation within me. It felt like a childhood Easter Sunday moving within my gut. All I knew is that it had been a really good day. As a matter of fact, it had been the best day I had experienced in a very, very long time.

I pulled the sheet over my eyes to block out the sunlight coming through the windows and fell immediately asleep, saying quietly to myself this time, "I am now a brand-new man."

CHAPTER 11

Shock and Awe, Lyle-Style

"...just as Christ was raised from the dead by the glory of the Father, we too might walk in newness of life." -Romans 6:4

Cautiously optimistic. That is how I would describe Scott's reaction when we finally met face-to-face so he could hear from me about what had happened a couple of days earlier. Scott was a thorough detective and asked for details about what was taking place inside me since my surrender. You need to recall that he had invested a couple of years going after my soul for Jesus, so he was not about to give me a premature high five on any decision I had made. Since that transformational moment, I had not had a sip of alcohol. Though there were drugs in my apartment from people that were still hanging out there, I had not smoked, snorted, or swallowed a thing. Almost humorously, for the remaining three months on my apartment lease, all I did was go to work, come home through the front door, and walk immediately to my bedroom, shutting my door behind me. On the other side of my bedroom wall, where friends and acquaintances would gather, there were still occurring all of the potentially corrupting activities that had been going on before my surrender to Jesus. The only difference was that I was no longer partaking. **Inwardly, the entire desire to get high had vanished. Literally, there was no inward compulsion to use drugs or drink. I was not even consciously restraining myself from using.** The decade long impulse to get high was taken from me in that moment of my surrender to Jesus. More than anything else, that was the clearest evidence that something significant had happened to me.

I still was not fully aware that I had been saved or that, because of that salvation, I now had the nature of Jesus living inside of me. I just kept finding recurring moments of shock and awe that an internal switch in me had somehow been flipped. The lone thing that I contributed was that

I intentionally stayed away from the presence of the drugs. Who knows whether or not I might have gotten sucked back into using had I not removed myself from the potential? Within a week of my deliverance, I found myself experiencing more pleasure reading the Bible than I had ever experienced getting drunk or high. My roommate and friends started getting a little annoyed that I was hiding out from them. I was not shy in telling them that I had "given my life to God" and would not be partying anymore. They laughed at me. They thought it was hysterical. We had all attempted to get clean over the years, and none of us had ever succeeded beyond a week or two. They believed this to be yet another lackluster attempt at Lyle sobering up. One of my friends, Carlos, with whom I once enjoyed theological debates while both of us were high on cocaine, called me one day to see what was up with me. He invited me to a bar, and I declined. I remember he got a little irritated with me and launched a pretty creative barrage of four-letter words at my newfound religious ways. He proclaimed over me that I would be back getting drunk and high with him in less than a month and that he would love to buy me my first shot of tequila. That was in 1994, and I can testify that I've neither been drunk nor high since August 2nd of 1994, two days before my conversion. Carlos had good reason to be skeptical, but his curse over me proved impotent.

Over the next several weeks, dozens of my old friends reached out to me. More than one told me that they missed me and wanted the old Jeff Lyle back. The more I read my Bible (I was up to eight to ten hours of reading a day at that point), the more I developed an understanding of the ways, words and works of Jesus. I grew in my capacity to explain myself theologically to my old friends. I was fairly convinced that I would be winning all of them to Jesus Christ in short order!

Everyone at work started seeing the changes too. A Christian lady there had heard from Scott what had happened to me, and I still remember her expression when I unloaded about a ten-minute testimony of what was going on with me. Because she knew what a terrible person I had been before that season, she was amazed at the Jesus-talk now coming out of me. By the way, my work ethic changed dramatically as a newly saved man. I showed up on time and stopped calling in sick. I worked harder than before and that caught the attention of my main boss. She was a very kind woman who was also a lesbian. The patience she had shown with me for the two years prior always endeared her to me. It was time for a performance review, and as she went over my most recent performance history, she affirmed that I was doing so much better. That opened the door in our performance review meeting for me to brag on Jesus as the One who deserved all the credit for the changes in my work ethic. In that little office, she stared at me across the conference table and told me that, for no other reason than the clear change in my attitude on the job, she was convinced that God had done something to me. I remember thinking that was awesome! **I had become a puzzling spiritual oddity at work and among my old friends.** They could not figure out what was going on with me. What had happened to Jeff Lyle? Not what. *Who.*

You may be wondering why I have not mentioned anything about going to church as a new follower of Jesus. That is coming, but it is connected to a much larger part of the story. Right now, I just want to throw down a little testimony about how people responded to the radical shift that the Father was facilitating in me. About a year before I was saved, I had dated a girl whom I will call Paige. She had gotten a hold of me at work about two months after I was delivered from the old life. We met up at a fast-food place to catch up on the last year and a half. Mind you, my whole drive during this season was to win souls for Jesus. My approach was really rough, more like an Old Testament, turn-or-burn prophet than the Gentle Shepherd who was leading me. I was a sincere witness of Christ, but I was fairly abrasive in what I said and how I said it. I operated with more gristle than grace when telling others about Jesus. With Paige, though, it was a little different. I calmly told her about how bad the drugs got in the months before I met the Savior. She understood as that was one of the main reasons she had kicked me to the curb when she broke things off with me. When I explained the moment of my conversion to her, she got quiet.

I was just sitting there happy, eating my French fries, letting her pick the Gospel shrapnel out of her hair from the Jesus-grenades I was tossing her way. I remember her lighting up a cigarette (you could still smoke inside some Georgia restaurants back then) and just staring at me for a minute. She blew out her smoke and said through thinly veiled bewilderment, "Your face looks completely different now." She did not say I looked happier. She did not say I was suddenly more handsome. The only adjective she used was the word *different*. It was like she could not quite pinpoint just what was triggering her, but God was clearly working in her heart. She came to church with me a few times and even attended a church-wide picnic at one of our deacon's homes. I really wanted Paige to get saved, so we began spending much more time together. Eventually, a wise man in my church saw that there might be some danger if I continued to pursue a deepening reconnection with her. His counsel caught me off guard, but because he was older, and because I did not wish to do anything to endanger my walk with Jesus, she and I agreed to part ways again. The last I heard is that she got married and had kids. I really wished I had gotten to see her get saved. God's grace is immense, and that older man told me, "Jeff, the Father cares more for her soul than you ever could. He has other witnesses out there. You pursue Jesus right now. He will pursue Paige."

Ultimately, in what was an excruciating test for me, God called me to walk away from all of my old friends. That sounds harsh but they were all still operating in a world to which I no longer belonged. I was not drinking or doing drugs, but my friends were like family to me. I continued for a couple of months after being saved to go shoot pool at the bars with them. It was only about once a week whereas it had previously been daily before I met Jesus. I remember going to my formerly favorite bar, wearing a shirt and tie after a Sunday evening church service. I had a couple of friends at the bar and they were more than a little shocked to see me there dressed as I was. I had that big blue Bible with me too. I set it on the bar and initiated a straight to the point conversation about their need to repent of their sins and commit themselves to Jesus Christ. As you can imagine, that went over about as well as a porcupine in a punchbowl at a wedding reception. To put it lightly, those two fellows and the bartender asked me to saturate that place with my absence. It was not a great moment for the advance of the Kingdom.

One week later, in a different bar where I was shooting pool, the Holy Spirit showed up. He was not there in that moment for the salvation of sinners. **He showed up to call me out of that place.** In a snapshot memory that I can still envision with clarity, the Holy Spirit allowed all of my physical senses to get overloaded in a span of about sixty seconds. With my eyes, I suddenly saw that there were lusty posters of half-naked women on the walls, a man wearing a tee shirt with a gigantic stenciled marijuana leaf on it, alongside the words **Gotta Smoke?** My sense of smell suddenly picked up the stench of urine, marijuana, cigarette smoke, beer, liquor, and some really cheap perfume that had been heavily doused by some really cheap-looking women (sorry, but them's the facts!). What served as the catalyst for me leaving, however, was **what I heard**. In addition to the nonstop cursing and the taking of the name of God in vain, playing over the speakers and being sung by some in the bar was the song called Straight to Hell by the old rock group *Drivin' N' Cryin'*. Here is what was being pumped through my hearing and into my mind that evening:

> *I'm going straight to Hell*
> *Just like my mama said*
> *I'm going straight to Hell*

Just months before, I had loved that song. I sang it at the top of my lungs, filled with margaritas and misery in the very bar where I now stood in front of a billiards table. The song was actually theologically accurate when I had formerly sung it. **Now it was no longer true about me**. The Holy Spirit whispered to me, "This is no longer the life I have for you. It is not enough that you aren't participating in drugs and drunkenness, Jeff. Your casual presence here in this place is endorsing all that you see, smell, and hear. There is no longer any fellowship for you in this place. You no longer belong here. Let's go home."

65

It is still bittersweet for me to acknowledge that, within a year of my conversion, I had almost zero ongoing contact with any of the people who had been such a huge part of my former life. I pulled back. Eventually, we all stopped returning each other's phone calls. Our paths had diverged and the one assigned to me was too narrow for them. Theirs was too broad for me. I miss some of them. Paul, especially. I heard later that he was particularly hurt when I decided that I could no longer run alongside him. We had been best friends in our years of mutual lostness. Carlos, the friend who falsely predicted that I would be getting drunk with him within weeks of my so-called conversion, died a few years later of alcohol-related physical complications. One of my dearest friends from those days who was like a sister to me, Kristin, died the same way. I conducted her funeral among old friends that I had not seen in a very long time. Though my other closest comrade, Jeff, had some genuine spiritual breakthroughs later in his life, I had the sad occasion of officiating his funeral after he passed away one night at home. I loved that dude. He and I connected at a heart level that neither of us understood nor had the ability to invest in when we were kids. Jeff struggled, but I am convinced that His conversion to Christ was genuine and that Jeff truly encountered the forgiveness of the Father through faith in Jesus. He and his grandfather came to see me at the church one day, and in broken trust, Jeff cried out to Jesus for forgiveness and life. He was spiritually alive, but I did not know enough to show him how to walk out that spiritual life with Jesus. *I miss my friend.* I miss all of them and still pray for many of them today to experience an awakening similar to the one which found and changed me.

Along with Carlos and Kristin, I buried a couple of other friends who never made it out of that cold prison of addiction. I mourned for each of them. My guess is that there will be more in the future whose caskets or urns will be placed in front of me as I share again that the only answer for any of us remains a Jewish preacher who lived and died and rose again in ancient Israel. For me, **Jesus is not my religion**. He is my rescuer and my friend. He is, more than anything, the living Lord of glory who has deep compassion for those who find themselves lost, afraid, addicted, and impossibly stuck. Jesus is still the Friend to sinners.

My friends and coworkers witnessed my life changing in those early days of walking with Jesus, and they thought the transformation that they were seeing was simply *shock-and-awe-Lyle-style*.

If they had only known it wasn't Lyle.

It was and still is Jesus.

CHAPTER 12
Do I Have to Go to Church?

"And day by day, attending the temple together and breaking bread in their homes, they received their food with glad and generous hearts, praising God and having favor with all the people. And the Lord added to their number day by day those who were being saved."
– Acts 2:46-47

GROWING UP IN THE SOUTHERN USA, going to church on Sundays was just part of the rhythms of the culture. I did not much care for it, to be honest. My dad enjoys recounting a story of me as a three-year-old, disrupting a service at First Baptist of Atlanta one morning during a Charles Stanley sermon. Apparently, we were sitting toward the top of the balcony, so we looked down at an angle at pretty much everything going on in the sanctuary. A few rows in front of my family, I am told, there was a bald man who was utilizing the comb-over method in an attempt to deceive us into believing he had a full head of hair. To my young eyes, all I saw was a thin dark line of hair running at an angle across an otherwise bald and shiny head. That is how bald men rolled back in the early 1970s. I did not comprehend what I was gazing upon, so I decided to tell my dad what I believed was happening with this man. Standing up on the pew, I pointed enthusiastically at the thin, dark strand of hair on his head, and I thundered as a prophet of truth, "DADDY! THAT MAN HAS A CRACK IN HIS HEAD!" I am confident that most of the Baptists around us that morning were not amused at my proclamation. *My dad thought it was awesome.* That should have been viewed as a precursor to me always feeling like a bit of a misfit in local churches. I ended up being a denominational mutt in my childhood. Baptist, Church of Christ, Alliance and the Christian Church were among the flavors of church life that I tasted. My experiences were never bad. I just did not get it. When the communion cracker tray was passed to me on the pew at Tucker Christian Church, I remember telling the usher, "No thanks. I'm not hungry." **There was a clear Kingdom disconnect in me.** I loved VBS and summer camps, but all the Sunday sermons were boring to me. What I was unaware of is that the Father was layering my heart with biblical truths via some kind of Kingdom *osmosis*. It was getting in me, thin layer upon thin layer. When my parents split up, our church at that time in Lilburn treated our family situation with a less than gracious response. My dad was over it. He pulled us out of the local church and taught me and my sister the Bible at home for a while. Eventually, some awesome neighbors, Bill and Pat Potter, began taking me to church with them and it was there that I found that I actually enjoyed the family component of the local church. Sermons were boring, music was somewhat outdated, and the old people smelled funny, but there was a togetherness that I was attracted to. In the days of my physical family disintegrating, the reality of a church family appealed deeply to me. **I could belong somewhere.** Yet, somewhere along the way, during my dark and deceived teenage years, I adopted the common attitude that churches were full of hypocrites and that whatever organized religion was, it was somewhat akin to Bubonic plague. Ironically, the most enriching days of my childhood were found among church-going Christians. The devil is an accuser and liar, and all during my teenage years and early twenties, I drank his Kool-Aid, laced with contempt toward the local church and those duped Jesus followers in general. I believed that those smarmy, Bible-thumping Christians were a group I could do without, so I intentionally kept my distance. Then God had the sovereign audacity to come and save me, bringing me out of the darkness and into His light. Almost instinctually, as a newly saved young adult, I knew that there would need to be a place in my life for church again.

Scott was wise to take up the reins as a spiritual father with me, and he basically mandated that I go to a church right down the street from my apartment. His own church was forty minutes away, and he did not wish to risk the driving distance becoming an eventual deterrent to my faithful attendance. He told me about **Meadow Baptist Church**. The pastor there had been one of his professors at a small Bible college in our county. Not knowing any other Christians, I listened to Scott's counsel and mustered up the courage to attend a Sunday service a couple of weeks after I surrendered my life to the Lord.

Looking back on it now, it was somewhat comical on that first Sunday for me as a guest at Meadow. I pulled up on a sweltering August Sunday at 10:45 a.m. Service would start in fifteen minutes, and I was anxious about walking into this place by myself. In preparation for my formal unveiling, I had gone the day before and gotten seven inches of hair cut off the back of my head. If you were alive in the early 1990s, you may remember that a fairly common hairstyle for men was The Mullet – *business in the front, party in the back*. My hair on the day before going to Meadow Baptist Church reached about midway down my back when wet. To clean up a bit, I asked the barber to take seven inches off the back and to clean up the front so Jesus would think I looked nice the next day at church. I exited my little low-rider truck and walked into the church building with my button-up shirt tucked into my Walmart slacks that I had bought right after my haircut the previous day. I was feeling *very Christian* as I walked to the front porch of the church in my new clothes, sporting my glorious new hairdo and clutching my big, blue hardback King James Bible in my hand. Though I was glad to be there, my nerves started pulsing as I walked into a church for the first time in over a decade. Happily, I did not burst into flames as I crossed the threshold, and the smiling faces who greeted me set my heart at ease.

Immediately, I realized that I was one of the youngest people in the place. Everyone was kind and welcoming, but they seemed a little old. Truth be known, they were then not much older than I am now. I quickly took the open seat on the very back row of pews. About five minutes before the service began, a young guy about my age came and handed me a bulletin and gave me a firm handshake, telling me that he was pleased to meet me. I read through the bulletin and took note of things called Tuesday Visitation, an Ice Cream Social, Sunday School attendance numbers from the previous week, and an announcement about an upcoming Missions Conference. I had no idea what any of that meant, but it all sounded interesting to me.

You can attach ice cream to just about anything, and I will show up for it. More people started coming into the auditorium, and eventually, a large man in a suit stood at the podium and called us all to grab a hymnal to begin our time of worship.

I had spent the last decade listening to hard rock, Southern rock, classic rock, Heavy Metal, and the recent Grunge sound that had been coming out of Seattle for a couple of years before my conversion. **When the morning music kicked off with an old organ and a piano, I nearly lost my salvation.** Frankly, the music did not sound bad, it was just, well, *weird*. I knew none of the hymns we sang that day, so I struggled to participate. Amid all the foreign-sounding singing, I do remember feeling a strong sense of peace and happiness when they hit the third or fourth song. Those Baptists were singing loudly and enthusiastically, just like we used to do in the bars on karaoke night. Except, unlike the bars, in this church, there was hope, love, and joy in the atmosphere. The Sunday suits, dresses, and hats were not hindering whatever it was that was happening in my heart. The time for the sermon came, and I recall being a little disappointed that we had to stop singing. It only took one service for the sound of worshiping God to win over my heart. **I did not love the style of the music that morning, but I loved the One to whom we were singing.** This was something I could get used to. Before too long, I would later join the choir. There were even a few occasions the next year when I sang lead in a quartet of men. You will not ever see that happen again, but it was innocent, sincere, and sweet. I don't regret it, even if the people who had to listen to me sing do.

When Pastor Jack made his way to the pulpit that morning, he told us to open our Bibles to whatever passage he shared from that day. I could not tell you a thing about what he preached, but I remember it was like cold water to my thirsty soul. I was spiritually ravenous to learn about this God who had saved me, and I devoured everything the pastor said that morning. About forty-five minutes later, he closed the message and called people to come to the altar for prayer. I stayed put because I was not sure who was qualified to present themselves at an altar in a church. Lots of other people went forward and knelt down on the floor. People were crying. Other people stood while someone put a hand on their shoulder as they prayed for them. I watched like a little kid at the zoo for his first time. None of this made sense to me, but it was beautiful, and I hungered to know more. When we were dismissed, I got to shake the pastor's hand at the front door on the way out. He said, "You must be Jeff. Scott told me that you would be visiting today." Amazed that the man in charge would actually know my name, I was hooked. Church had been a surprisingly great experience for me that morning! I told him that I would be back the next Sunday to give Meadow Baptist Church an additional go.

What I never could have fathomed is that, just a little over eight years later, in that same building, the people of Meadow would vote to name me their Lead Pastor. The little boy who never quite treasured church-going, the teenage drug user who went to a youth gathering tripping on LSD, the young man who bought into the cultural cynicism about the local church, the newly saved guy who got seven inches of his hair cut off to gain some leverage with the Almighty, would be summoned by the Holy Spirit to dedicate his life to serving the King by serving His people in the local church. Pastor Jack baptized me in that church a few weeks later. It was in that church building where I would receive my call to ministry from the Holy Spirit just four months after that first visit. I preached my first sermon there. It was in that building that I met my future wife, and a year after we met, we were married there. My two children were born in the years during which we served in that sanctuary. There, in that very same room, I would be formally ordained before a crowd of two hundred people. Through scores of glorious and inglorious sermons released by me in that building, I learned the art of preaching. Who could have known what was to come? **Only God.** I was just showing up on that Sunday in August of 1994 to do what Scott told me to do. I was a Christian, and according to Scott, Christians went to church every Sunday. So, I showed up in obedience to what I had been told. Little did I know what the Lord would begin on that unassuming Sunday. My question from years gone by of, "Do I have to go to church?" became the joyful, stunned declaration of, "I get to serve the Church!"

The Father had truly given me a fresh start. I had spent those early childhood years before Him, never understanding that His eye had always been on me in love and faithfulness. Then came those long years when I was so far away from Him, choosing rebellion and rage. The unspeakable mercy shown to me brought me unto Him through a supernatural deliverance and cleansing. It was not enough for Him to bring me just unto Himself. He brought me unto His other children. He revealed the validity of the local church to me, even as I would grow more and more familiar with all of the flaws of Christian people. God had a place for me in His family. He called me to Himself *and* His people. From these deep movements in my life which came from the Father, He set me on a definite course where I learned what it meant to live *for Him*. This was a huge transition for me as one who had formerly known only what it meant to live for myself in aimlessness leading to emptiness. God brought me unto Himself by grace and then released something to me that I had never believed I would find: **my purpose in this world.**

SECTION 4

FOR HIM

CHAPTER 13

Learning to Wait

"And let us not grow weary of doing good, for in due season we will reap,
if we do not give up."
- Galatians 6:9

THE END OF 1994 AND the entire year of 1995 seemed to be like a dream to me. With my addictions forever gone and my mind being renewed by the Word and the Holy Spirit, I was experiencing the substance of what it meant to be born again. Everything was new to me. For the first time in my life, I was experiencing the leadership of God in my heart, and I was loving where He was continually leading me. Pastor Jack was a smart man, and he made good use of my zeal and availability. I still had four days off from my job every week, and I offered to use those days to do whatever I could do at the church. My schedule was changed to release me from nightshift and place me back on dayshift. Guess who was my new supervisor? None other than my friend, Scott! The man that had led me to Jesus could now mentor me as a new disciple. Those long hours side by side were resumed but this time with both of us as sons of God. I did my forty hours each week at work and then served God part-time at the church on my off days. Over time, Scott and I began to have an impact on our other coworkers in our department. Where we worked was notorious for being staffed with party people who were a wee bit rough around the edges. Soon, the Lord began to move, and we saw many of our coworkers come to Jesus or recommit their lives to Him. By the time Scott resigned his position to go full-time as the new pastor of a church in his city, our department was known more for the people's Christian zeal than it had ever been known for its heavy-duty partying. Yes, the Holy Spirit brought a mini revival over the course of 1995 and into 1996 to our department. The winds were blowing, and beautiful changes were being stirred all around us.

When Scott moved away from the company in 1996 to enter full time pastoring, it was bittersweet. He had become my best friend, and things would not be the same without him. God had been so good to me to allow me to be under his care for those two full years. When he left, I had been strengthened enough to lean upon the Lord on my own. I had my church family, my pastor, and a decent group of friends who were sharpening me in my walk with Jesus. **What I was not prepared for was the longing in my own heart to be free from my marketplace job and to enter into vocational ministry.** You see, God had called me to preach on Wednesday, December 14th, 1994 – just four months after my salvation. I answered that internal calling and immediately began preaching in the prisons, the homeless shelters, and the nursing homes. I was not yet skilled at any of it, but I was faithful to pray for God's help, and then to preach to the best of my ability whatever Bible passage God laid upon my heart. The more I did it, the more I longed to do it. My natural gift of communication was now being harnessed by the Spirit, and I soon learned the essence of what it meant to abide under an anointing to preach. To think that I once would have been thrilled to talk on the radio as a DJ – now, God was using me to speak life from His Word to people who were hungry to hear. Mercifully, God did not unleash my unrefined approach to preaching anywhere that would invite a broad audience. He left me in small venues where I could figure out things as I went, without inflicting too much damage on my captive audiences. Preaching in the jails every Monday night was a blast, and the prisoners had nothing better to do, so they were always happy to see me, even if my theology and skillset were not exactly precise. More than once, as the inmates entered the chapel, there were some stunned expressions on the faces of men to whom I had once sold drugs who were now inmates. *What is Lyle doing in here with a Bible in his hand?* More than a few of them eventually committed themselves to Jesus as it was impossible to deny the evidence of all the changes that He had worked in my life. I loved preaching in that jail. The feeling of speaking God's Word became such a treasure to me in those days. Yet, three days a week, for thirteen hours each day, it was back to the data center at work where I was reminded that I still was not fully free to pour my entire life into the ministry given to me.

Scott was gone.

I became inwardly unfulfilled at work.

Preaching the Word was my call from Heaven, not watching boring computer screens.

Frustration, impatience, weariness, and irritability began to root down in my heart.

I began to deeply resent my job.

Why could I not be full-time in ministry? I mean, after all, I had been *saved three whole years!*

My pastor and I had talked about bringing me on to the church full-time but he was not yet ready to pull the trigger on that privilege for me. Truthfully, I was not ready. God needed to purge me of all this nasty presumption in my heart. **Anyone who feels entitled to anything is not ready for whatever it is they feel entitled to.** God let me flounder in that data center for another eighteen months after Scott left. While I was still enjoying the ministries I had been assigned, I had lost a fair amount of my joy. Somehow, I had become critical, narrow, and fairly legalistic. More than once, I was corrected by older, wiser believers for coming off as being judgmental. Sourness had invaded my spirit, and I could not get out from under it. My attitude had ditched itself into an abyss. Over a period of about two months in late 1996, the Lord led me to a fresh repentance and surrender. I committed to God that I would serve Him joyfully, both at my job and in my church ministries. I surrendered my heart and told Him that I would choose joy and faithfulness, even if he left me at my job forever and never allowed me to enter full-time ministry. The next couple of months were refreshed, and I felt that my soul had been reoriented to a healthy place. In the Spring of 1997, my pastor asked to meet with me at the church. He invited me to leave my job and join him on staff as the Minister of Evangelism at Meadow Baptist Church. Two weeks later, I left the marketplace world and entered into vocational ministry. By God's grace, I did not quit hoping and believing during those days of discouragement and weariness. I learned the value of unquestioning obedience and diligent servanthood. Most of all, I passed God's class called *Good Attitude 101.*

It took a while, and I flunked some of the periodic quizzes, but when all was said and done, I passed His class. He made me wait. He refused to open the door for me to enter into the privilege of vocational ministry prematurely. He let me stew in my own juices until I got sick of them. A few months after my surrender of my job to the Lord, my dream came true, and I set up my personal cubicle in the church office. At twenty-seven years old, with three years of sobriety and deliverance under my belt, my early dream of serving God vocationally came true. **I am so very glad that He taught me to wait on His timing**. It would be a skill that I would need to employ time and time again.

Some of you reading my testimony about the waiting season are being called to do what I had to do. It is my conviction now that God makes everyone whom He loves and uses to wait upon Him. He intentionally takes us to the limits of our patience. He confronts our restlessness and our impulse to be the ones who are in charge. Clocks and calendars become instruments of torture for us in those seasons. We feel it is illogical to wait any longer. Frustration talks us into discouragement, discouragement tries to talk us into quitting or making something happen in our own timing. As the Holy Spirit lovingly confronts us with this weakness in us, we start hearing the voice of the Father who deeply loves us.

He repeatedly asks us if we still trust Him.

He refuses to bow to our timelines.

When we finally get still and begin to intentionally listen to Him again, we start learning some very important things about what it means to follow Jesus as a disciple. **We learn that He is much more focused on the journey than He is the arrival.**

God knows that He can get you to where He wants us at the perfect time. He never obsesses over how quickly He can make things happen. Jesus likes the waiting process because it is during those times that He takes greater ownership of our hearts. We learn *His accent* during times of enforced waiting. We are made aware by the Holy Spirit how precious it is just to be with Jesus, even if He is standing still while the clock is ticking, and the calendar is turning. The bottom line is that God is never in a hurry. That is our disease, not His. So, if you are in that smothering season of feeling stuck in a place where time has stopped, take a moment and look for Jesus there. What does He have for you in this place of situational molasses from which you are unable to extract yourself? What is He saying to you about Himself? About you? I can promise you that there is a reason why the door *into the next* has not opened yet. It is not because Jesus is ignoring you, disinterested in what you feel, or cruel in His response to you. It is because there is still something within your current reality with which He seeks to mature and equip you. He is actually giving you something precious that you are unable to receive on the run. He requires you to remain still. He is massaging your heart surrender to rise to a new level. He wants your refined trust of Him to begin to pulse more strongly in your veins. The clock and the calendar do not love you. They will betray you if you bow down to serve them. Jesus always has your greatest good in mind. Your waiting is for Him – not merely upon Him, but *for* Him. Unto Him. In honor of Him.

That is why you are waiting. By faith, believe it now. Soon enough, it will all become clear to you. When it does, you will humbly, sincerely, and joyfully thank Him for making you wait. **I was figuring that out as I went.**

CHAPTER 14
The One: A Girl Named Amy

"He who finds a wife finds a good thing and obtains favor from the Lord."
- Proverbs 18:22

HEY, ALL YOU UNMARRIED READERS – listen up! The Apostle Paul writes in 1st Corinthians 7:6-7 of an empowerment from God that will enable certain Christians to remain unmarried. I remember reading that shortly after being saved, and as a single young man, I felt a strong inclination to erase those verses out of my Bible. It sounded to me like a threat from Heaven that God might arbitrarily choose to *gift me* with the absence of a wife for the rest of my days. I did not want to be single! I wanted a woman! I needed a wife! Later, I learned a little more in-depth that those whom God calls to remain single and celibate are actually given an enablement from the Holy Spirit to happily live without a spouse. **I did not have that gift nor did I want it!** From 1994 until the fall of 1996, my eyes were scanning the horizon almost nonstop to locate the lovely lady that would eventually become Mrs. Lyle. The way things worked at our church was that the older ladies felt an admixture of love and pity for a young, single preacher who still had not found a bride. It was not uncommon for one of the surrogate moms or grandmothers who had adopted me to introduce me to a daughter, niece, granddaughter, third-cousin twice removed, female weight lifter, short-order cook, or cashier at the gas station with the possibility that she might become my wife. There were no shortages of opportunities, and I tried to be as polite as I could with all the introductions and suggestions, but I knew with each of them that, whoever she was at that moment, she was not *the one*. I was eventually introduced to a young lady that I really thought was going to become my wife. So did most of the people at our church which added a little congregational grapevine element into the mix. Six months later, it became evident that the Lord had other plans for both of us. She moved away and I was left at the church, going

82

in and out of struggling to process just how it is that a Christian man is supposed to locate the singular woman out of the three billion or more who were on planet earth at that time. In the weeks after our breakup, I got really serious with the Lord as I was forced to confess that I was completely ignorant about how to approach the art of receiving from Him the woman with whom I would spend the rest of my life.

As He normally does with me, the Holy Spirit led me into an adventure of searching the Scriptures to see what God valued in a woman. As I begin to methodically go through the Scriptures, a picture of who I was looking for began to be formed. If I could just locate the lady that was being defined by my Bible, I was going to find the wife whom God had set aside for me. Here is what I learned about who she would be, and the Scripture references which God used to enlighten me:

1. **She needed to be saved and deeply committed to Jesus (2ⁿᵈ Corinthians 6:14)**
2. **She needed to be willing to follow my loving leadership of her (Ephesians 5:22-24)**
3. **She needed to be respectable, self-controlled, trustworthy, and able to regulate her patterns of verbal communication (1ˢᵗ Timothy 3:11)**
4. **She needed to be governed inwardly by a meek and quiet spirit, which God declares that he finds extremely valuable in His daughters (1ˢᵗ Peter 3:14)**
5. **I needed to be physically attracted to her. The Bible has plenty to say about sex, and marital intimacy should never be deprioritized simply because most people mistakenly see it as merely physical or emotional, but not necessarily spiritual.**
6. **She needed to love Jesus more than she loved me. Apart from that, she could not love me as I needed to be loved.**

While there was much more to my quest to know how to recognize the woman who would become my wife, I felt that these six qualities would empower me to search with a biblically informed heart, and also rule out the vast majority of young women that I was being introduced to in those days. **For any and all of you who are unmarried, I really want to encourage you to make the search for your mate a proactive partnership between you and the Holy Spirit.** Just because he or she looks attractive and goes to church DOES NOT mean that you have found Mr. or Ms. Right(eous). Emotions are awesome, and they should be a healthy part of all marriages, but your emotions must never be the foundation of your search for your future spouse. The devil has plenty of people who can hit Level 10 on the Tingle-Meter for you. Ladies, Mr. Cool may have lips of butter…but a heart of horseradish. Guys, I appreciate the fact that the first time you saw her gorgeous self, your eyes vacated their sockets and rolled on to the floor, but the most essential parts of her are buried beneath everything that you see on the outside. Many Christians sadly adopt the approach that the carnal world system offers when it comes to finding a spouse. God wants to partner with you for as long as it takes to bring you and your future mate together. He wants to be right in the midst when you two meet one another.

As these realities began to gain traction in my own heart those many years ago, I remember telling the Father one day while praying, "Lord, I do not know how to find the right woman. That much is clear. I am asking You to let me know who she is. I will not romantically give any part of my heart to anyone else until I know that You sent her."

Just a few months after praying that prayer and remaining fully committed to my part in it, I showed up at church to lead the Young Singles Class that I was teaching on that particular Sunday while the couple that normally led it were out of town. There were only about fifteen of us in the class each week, but we had become a fairly tight group of friends. On this particular morning, there was a new face in the class. I noticed that face. *I liked that face.* She was beautiful, and she radiated joy on her countenance. *Who was the new girl?* What really piqued my curiosity was that, as I was teaching, she had her Bible open on her lap and found every passage of Scripture that I referenced. She nodded her head at the awesomely masterful points in my gloriously crafted Sunday School lesson. After the class concluded,

I introduced myself formally and found out that she was Amy Samples from Alpharetta, a city about twenty-five minutes from our church. The next Sunday, she was back. I must admit that I was hoping she would be and that I was keeping my eye out for her. There was something about this Amy that intrigued me, but I was intentionally keeping a healthy approach in motion so that nothing in my heart was moved toward her before God gave me some form of permission to engage her. **I had figured out a few things as I went.**

Over the next few weeks, I learned a little more about Amy. She was connected by family to a local pastor for whom I had preached a few times. His sister had married Amy's grandfather after Amy's grandmother died several years before. He knew I was a single preacher who was praying about a wife, so he may have dropped a few hints in my favor after they learned that Amy was attending Meadow Baptist Church. Amy went to a Southern Baptist church in Roswell with her whole family, including aunts and uncles. She sang for Jesus there at the church and was formally trained in music theory. She enjoyed playing piano on the side but was more comfortable singing harmony in ensembles and trios. Additionally, I found out that the only reason Amy ever showed up at Meadow Baptist in the first place was that, the week before I met her in our single's group, she had been traveling to another church to attend service. She got lost on our city's roads that day and found herself at a traffic light right at 11:00 a.m. when churches typically began their services. Rather than walking her introverted self into the other church late, if and when she found it, she just decided to attend the church right in front of her on the other side of the traffic light. That church just happened to be Meadow. **God was listening to my prayers and working silently to do something that I never could have made happen on my own.** He was bringing me a wife from Alpharetta!

As the weeks went by, Amy eventually felt led by the Father to leave her parents' church and join Meadow. She and I were simply friends who were becoming better friends. Though I thought she was beautiful and really respected her walk with the Lord, it was not something that either of us would define as love at first sight. We were taking our time. Amy had just come out of a failed relationship that was similar to the one that ended for me a few months before I met her. I watched her join our choir and make fast friends with lots of people. Our singles group would go out to eat after church and do some occasional fun stuff as a group. I was watching and observing this lovely creature. My six priorities for a future wife seemed to be regularly being fulfilled with Miss Amy Samples. Not surprisingly, a few of the other single guys in the group were taking notice of her too. *Was that a twinge of jealousy I was feeling?* Eventually, I went and talked to the man who taught our single's class each week. He and his wife had become close to Amy, and I wanted to pick his brain about what he thought. It was almost as if he was waiting for an opportunity to tell me what a great lady he thought Amy was. His wife agreed. About a week after that discussion, I felt like I had permission from the Lord to ask her out on a date. To keep it as low-key as possible, we made it a double date with my friend and his wife. Amy agreed to accompany me on our first date to…*wait for it*…Captain Billy's Fish House. On Fridays, the fine folks at Captain Billy's would have a Southern Gospel group to sing while their patrons ate. Can it get any better than that? Some fried catfish, hushpuppies, coleslaw, and twangy Jesus music being performed by a live Gospel group.

It's hard to believe I ever got a second date with her.

The next couple of months were great. Amy and I continued to date lightly. I met her family, including her dad who was 6'8" and a wee bit intimidating. Her mom was gentle and sweet. I loved Deborah from the first day I met her. Aunt Darlene and Uncle Rupert hosted all of us at their home, and Darlene's gregarious demeanor kept things light. Amy's dad took me aside and illustratively warned me about what could happen to me if I ever brought any hurt to his daughter. I won't go into details, but it involved an egg being gripped in his enormous hands. *Message received Mr. Samples.*

Our first Valentine's Day rolled around, and we still had not really formalized the status of our relationship. We were more than friends, but we had not come out and declared that we were exclusively belonging to one another. She still reminds me to this day that I signed her Valentine's Day card that year with "Your Friend, Jeff Lyle." Now you are clearly seeing that it was only God who ever turned this relationship into an eventual marriage with two children! Two months later, Amy called me to read to me over the phone an unsigned love letter she had received in the mail from an anonymous man who, based on what was written in the letter, clearly went to our church. Talk about awkward. Here I was, wondering if this girl was going to eventually be *the one*, and she was reading me some other dude's bad poetry who was aiming to win her heart. When she got done, I felt it was make-or-break time for me. I believe my exact words to her were, *"Uh, Amy, I don't know who this guy might be, but, well, uh...you're kinda spoken for."*

I did it!

I put myself out there, and I let her know that Mr. Invisible Romeo the Poet should have no further access to her because she and I were now officially a couple if she would agree to it. She felt the same, and so, from that day forward, things picked up momentum. While I remained a bit of a stumbler in conveying my feelings for her, in April of that year, for the very first time we told each other, "I love you." This was it. It felt so good to know that I was dating a lady whom I might be given the joy of marrying.

I prayed and fasted about next steps. Heaven was silent. I talked to my pastor. He agreed to pray for us but had no indication either way if Amy Samples was the one for me. The Lord seemed to be shutting down all other voices who might help me discern if I could pop the question to my new girl. Interestingly, once people found out that we were exclusively dating one another, lots of voices began speaking *to Amy about me*. The consensus seemed to be *"Run, Amy, run!"* I am still not exactly sure why others did not want her to be with me, but their little strategies to separate us failed miserably as we became more and more clear on what was happening between us. In those days, I did not have the appropriate vocabulary for what was happening with us. I would say now that the Holy Spirit was orchestrating a merger that would become a marriage. All the prayers of Amy, me, our parents, and our brothers and sisters in Christ were in the process of being answered as the Lord inched us closer to becoming husband and wife.

> *But Heaven still had not clearly spoken with permission about the next steps. I was getting restless within.*

Honestly, I was confident in my heart that we would be getting married, but I had committed to the Lord to wait upon Him. I had begun well in my approach to pursuing Amy. God had been honored. I had also intentionally honored Amy the whole time treating her as the lady that she clearly was and treasuring her as a prized daughter of God. Now that it was getting down to the wire for me, there was a temptation to *assume* God was fine with me proposing to her. I withstood the temptation for a few more weeks. Then, on a Sunday morning after my pastor finished preaching, I went down to the altar to pray. I heard the inner voice of the Holy Spirit say to me, **"You don't have to look anymore. You don't need to pray about marrying her anymore. She is the one."**

That was on a Sunday. I went the following Wednesday and purchased an engagement ring. I called Mr. Samples and asked to meet with him and, when we met, I asked permission to propose to Amy. He strung me out for a bit, but he eventually smiled and said that he would be pleased with his daughter marrying me if she desired to do so. Not one to waste time, I asked Amy to dinner for the Friday night of the following week. We went to Little Gardens restaurant in my hometown of Lilburn, and there I asked Amy Samples if I could have the honor of making her my wife.

She said yes. The beautiful, joyful, Jesus-loving Amy Samples was the one. God was going to let me belong to her as her husband. He had chosen to gift me with her as my wife. Euphoria hit me in those days. We were going to be married!

Almost six months later to the very day, Amy and I became husband and wife in the sanctuary of Meadow Baptist Church. The place was packed, and the wedding ceremony included a full Gospel quartet, a twenty-minute sermon from my pastor so that my unsaved friends who were in attendance would hear the message of Jesus, and then a reception with a couple hundred people out in the fellowship hall. We spent our first night as husband and wife in a suite at a local high-rise hotel before heading off to our honeymoon week in the mountains together. **I had no idea how to be a husband but was so happy that I would be figuring it out as I went forward with Amy as my better half.** You will learn much more about Amy later in this book, but I want to be clear when I affirm that she is the perfect woman for me. She was so worth the wait. The longer we have been married, the more I admire, respect, and love that woman. Through some tragic events, I would find that Amy is not just a good wife for me, but she is a good woman for the glory of God. Beauty, wisdom, courage, and tenacity mark this daughter of God. I'll share more about her – this woman about whom so many still sense an undefinable mystique – later, but I want to begin to weave together some major strands that have been independent of one another up to this point. As Amy and I began our newly married lives together, ministry would come steamrolling in at a high rate of speed, bringing with it some incredible blessings and some undesirable burdens.

I was now living **for Him** with the responsibilities of a husband, a soon-to-be-father, a young pastor, and a man who was going to have his crutches kicked out from under him by a Divine foot. That's right, God was about to initiate a long season wherein He would expose all my props and call me into the deep divide that falls between living *for* God and living *with* God.

CHAPTER 15

A Chapter of Confessions

"...for he was marvelously helped, till he was strong."
– 2 Chronicles 26:15

IS ANYONE ELSE OCCASIONALLY PERTURBED that time travel has not yet been invented? That missing piece of human history is long overdue in my opinion. Along with the absence of a pill that will completely solve my male pattern baldness, the lack of ability to turn back the clock is something that one of you really smart people need to go ahead and make happen. If I could go back in time to the years between 1997 and 2000 and redo some things, I think my life would have contained far fewer breakdowns and blowups. If you have never been a man in his twenties, allow me the privilege of letting you know a few of the curses that are attached to being young, empowered, and male. Here are those blind spots in no particular order:

1. **Operating simultaneously with a surplus of confidence and a deficit of wisdom.**
2. **Formulating answers to questions that nobody is asking, and indiscriminately releasing them as if they were chunks of gold to enrich all with whom we come into contact. This is also known as "the ignorance of our arrogance."**
3. **Finding something at which we are skillful, investing the best of ourselves there, and then neglecting or ignoring all of the other things in which we are not necessarily excelling. Young men typically play to their strengths while dismissing their deficiencies.**
4. **If we happen to be Christian young men, memorizing all the Bible verses that wives need to make sure to obey while conveniently doing in-depth Greek and Hebrew word studies**

to explain away all the verses that God requires husbands to know, believe, and obey.

5. If the young man is in vocational ministry, placing most things in life in an orbit around the unprecedented, astounding Kingdom works we are doing for the Lord.

Before I get any more embarrassed, let me just leave you with those five things. Believe me, there are dozens more blind spots and blowouts that are connected to being young, empowered, and male. We might simply put most of them under the umbrella of the word *cocky*. I would love to tell you that I escaped all or most of these common faults when I was young, but there are too many witnesses who are still alive that could refute that testimony. So, let me go ahead and write this as a chapter of my confessions.

When Amy and I returned from our honeymoon, we came home to the parsonage on the church property to begin our lives together. Amy had never lived apart from her parents, and ours was the first home that was hers to create as her own nest. While we were away on our honeymoon, she had her dad and brother paint our bedroom a deep pink color – *kind of like a baboon's rear end*. At least, that is the way it impacted me when I walked into it. I had been a bachelor for nearly ten years before our wedding. There had never been any true decor in any of the places where I had lived as a single man. The only pink thing that had ever been in one of my apartments or houses were the white socks that I accidentally washed with a red shirt. *I did not do pink.* My new reality, however, was filled with constant visual reminders that a woman was now calling the shots concerning what our home looked like. Gone was my black, cast-iron bed frame with the treasured black comforter that I had slept under for years. Somebody had painted my formerly black bed glossy white and placed it in the baboon-bottom-deep-pink bedroom. Additionally, there was now a floral comforter spread across it. There were extra pillows that sat upon the bed, and they were also florally patterned. I was not to place my head upon these pillows. They were to be set aside at bedtime. They were merely there for decor. *Who knew such things existed?* I remember that there was also a standing bunny rabbit in a blue-jean jumper in the corner of the bedroom. This, I was informed, was also decor. My bathroom was no longer mine – a garden had invaded it by way of a female hand orchestrating trinkets, pictures, and faux foliage. More flowers and gardens were hanging in framed pictures all along our walls throughout the entire home. Our dishes even matched. Drinking glasses were actually made of glass and not plastic. The silverware was now organized in a tray instead of being in a heap in the kitchen drawer. Garbage cans were now hidden from plain sight and the ironing board was to be put away after each usage. Not wanting to sound like a complainer, I will happily confess that I was deeply pleased **that there was also now food** in the refrigerator and the pantry. I got to eat at home instead of in my car as had been my perpetual habit since I was in my late teens. That part was cool. The rest of the changes, however, were things I had to adjust to in order to keep peace. My pastor told me, "The house is hers. Get used to it. You pay for it; she tells you where things go."

I was now living in a house with a wife and learning that the woman therein hath dominion.

While it truly was a shock to my senses, I acclimated over time, and like most men, I failed to even notice all the new visuals in our home after the second month of us living there. My focus was on my ministry and upon all the territory that was out there for me to conquer in the name of King Jesus. Looking back, I was wholly unaware of the needs in Amy's heart, and I did not find out until much later how difficult it was for her to step into a life that did not provide any clarity for her role, value, and priorities as a woman or wife. Like many young husbands, I subconsciously operated as if I had merely added a wife to my pre-existing life. *She was to help me. She was to take care of the home. She was to encourage and support me as I went off to war for the glory of the King.* Far from loving her like Jesus loves the Church, I took her for granted without being aware of it. Little did I know that, even at that early stage in our marriage, Amy and I began running on parallel tracks that rarely crossed. Please know that we never fought. There was not a whole lot of tension. We actually had a good bit of fun, but she was lonely in her marriage to me from almost the get-go. Fortunately, her mom and her aunts were a huge part of her life, and they filled the gaps in which I failed to invest. Amy and I were husband and wife, but we were not deepening friends yet since becoming husband and wife. I was still living with my relational walls up, all the while being completely ignorant that anything was missing in our marriage. **Amy carried our marriage for years.** My guess is that there are a lot of rewards awaiting her in Heaven that are connected to her diligence in those challenging days. My role at the church was producing some visible results as the membership numbers grew, and momentum was increasing among the congregants. I got to sit on the platform next to my pastor every Sunday in one of those big Baptist thrones that so many churches utilized in those days. If I am being honest, I was enjoying a season wherein everything I touched turned to gold. My pastor was happy with me, the people I helped lead were supportive and encouraging, and I went home across the parking lot every day to a beautiful, faithful, and dutiful woman who made me feel pretty awesome about myself. While I was operating at a high level of ministry capacity, my relational skills with Amy were lacking. I am not sure how she endured those first three years by my side. If I could use one descriptor to characterize those early years with her, I would hang over them a banner that declared that I was operating in **relational ignorance, marital negligence, and subtle arrogance**. While I was drawing my validity from my ministry, Amy had to press more deeply into the Lord. I tell people to this very day that my wife is a stronger Christian than I am. Nobody debates me about that. Part of the reason why this is true is that, while I leaned on the crutch of what I was producing in ministry for God, Amy leaned hard upon God Himself.

I need to confess something else, too. During those years, was a spreading disease in my soul. I had learned to live by a code, a formula, and a religious checklist. Without even knowing it, I had embraced a prostituted version of Christianity called **legalistic fundamentalism**. The rebel who had been — redeemed now had become externally religious. My spiritual disciplines became a source of religious pride to me. I awoke each day at around

4:00 a.m. I read my Bible for an hour or two. Next, I would pray for an hour as I was trained to do. I can recall there were times where I would pause my prayer on my floor, open one eye to glance at the clock and calculate how many minutes were left before my sixty minutes of praying were complete. Fasting was part of how I believed I earned favor with God. When my appointed day of finishing a fast arrived, I would set my alarm for 12:01 a.m. on the next day so I could get up and eat something.

Some of my mentors had taught me that I needed to have my hair a certain length. I should never have a mustache or beard. Godly women always wore skirts (well below the knee) or dresses. Movie theaters and the filth within them were barely one step removed from the culture of Hell's abyss itself. If you ever had a social drink, it was clear evidence that you had never been born again. Then there was the informal membership that I held in the King James Only Cult. Any other translation of the Bible was not a real version, but a *perversion*. I remember saying in a sermon one time that, if you listened to non-Christian music, you absolutely forfeit God's touch on your life. My little code ballooned to near pharisaical proportions. The list was always growing, and I was not hesitant to measure others by it. By God's grace, though this season in my life was intense and obnoxious, it was not prolonged. **My precious mother-in-law, Deborah Samples, was soon to be used by God to gently usher me out of legalism and into liberty.** Until that day arrived, however, I was one smug young minister. Truthfully, we all were. Both older and younger pastors in our denomination could strut while still sitting down. It is truly embarrassing now for me to think of how I once expressed my faith. God had to save me out of my religion just as He had to save me out of my former rebellion.

Religious pride, in my opinion, has a far worse stench than outright rebellion against God. Rebels aren't pretending. Legalists live in a fantasyland that puffs them up daily with performance-driven pride. To this day, I spiritually gag when I am around it. It is stunning that I could not see it in myself when I was living in it. It is similar to how you don't feel wet when you are underwater. Truly, God was going to have to save me a second time. The first deliverance was from my years of overt rebellion. The second time would be a salvation from my proud stint in man's religion.

Those long years of rebellion had driven some deep scars into me as an unsaved man. No less threatening to me as a saved man was this legalistic trajectory I had found. In Jesus' parable in Luke 15:11-32, we find two sons that were distanced from their father. One was a flagrant sinner who lived in open dishonor, treating his father with arrogant indifference. He is the son that most people remember from the parable. Yet, the other son was also living outside of his father's desire.

> The other son kept all the rules.
> He stayed in geographical closeness to his father.
> He worked hard and strived to do things which affirmed that he was a good boy.

When his rebellious young brother returned home in repentance to their father, the older brother was angry because he did not feel celebrated by his dad. His rule-keeping had been his justification, and the father did not seem to offer enough affirmation to him for all his *do-gooder* efforts. This older brother represents legalistic, fundamentalist religion in the parable. I did not see it then, but it was certainly true that **I had moved from my rebellion into my religion**. In my deep sins, I had lived for myself. In my committed religion, I was still living for myself. I was seeking to prove my worth as a son of God. Some of you may believe that this was still better than embracing a lifestyle of sin. Perhaps, in some practical ways, it could be. Yet, religious pride is often more difficult to repent from than profligate rebellion. I was not yet thirty years old, and I had already lived the lives of both sons in Jesus' parable. Neither of those sons really knew or loved their dad. They both used him, but neither boy had relational closeness with him. My legalistic ways made me feel like I knew the Father, but I really didn't. I knew so much about Him from reading His book, but when I could not do something for Him that was good, I felt anxious. When I failed Him, I felt terrified because my foundation for relating with Him was based almost entirely on my daily performance as His servant. **When He tried to tell me that I was His beloved boy, all I heard was that I was His appreciated servant.** It would be a few more years until I really began to hear His whispers over me concerning my sonship. Eventually, I would learn the accent of the Almighty. Until then, my striving would be my comfort – always working for what I already possessed. Rest was for the irresponsible Christian. Those men and women would never amount to much. They did not know how important it was to redeem the time before the Second Coming. As for me, I would outrun them. Everyone should just sit back and watch. In a world full of *Clark Kents* in the Church, it was time for them to behold their Superman. Off came my horn-rimmed glasses, and on came my red cape of competency in the Kingdom. I was going to fly far and high for Jesus.

At least that is what I believed at the time, but the Father had some Kryptonite reserved for me a little way down the road. There was still so much for me to figure out as I went.

CHAPTER 16

Bringing Home Babies

*"Behold, children are a heritage from the LORD, the fruit of the womb a reward. –
Psalm 127:3*

WHEN AMY TOLD ME THAT she was pregnant, I was so happy. We had tried for a couple of months to conceive, and I remember the rush that filled my own heart when she giddily showed me the pregnancy test. We were now three years into our marriage and becoming incrementally closer with one another in our married life. While Amy would share with me much later that these were still very hard years for her as a wife, we had embraced a marital rhythm that served us well enough as we awaited breakthrough in our marriage. She still had her mom and aunts to supply her with companionship, a listening ear, and sympathetic hearts. I was still cheating on Amy with my mistress named *Ministry*. There was so much grace still being showered on us from a Father who was bringing us closer to Him. We had talked a good bit about being parents, and though I did not exactly feel confident that I was ready, I really wanted a child. In fact, I specifically wanted *a daughter*. Though I was operating at a high level of ignorance about much of my relational struggles, I did possess the insight that God could use a sweet little baby girl to soften some of my emotional intensity. My concern was that I might be too hard on a boy if we received a son as our firstborn. So, I prayed for a baby girl, and we soon got the news from Amy's sonogram that this would become our reality. **In July of 2000, my dreams came true as I watched Amy bring our daughter, Alicia, into the world through a long, painful labor.** I wept as I witnessed the miracle of Alicia's birth in real time. Instant was my love for this child! Alicia was actually the very first baby I had ever held in my arms. Love had never really come easily for me, but with my newborn daughter, it was instant and effortless. We took her home from the hospital a few days later and welcomed her into her beautiful *Winnie The Pooh* themed nursery that our friend, Jennifer, put together for us in the parsonage. As with every set of new parents, there was a learning curve. Diapers were fun for the first couple of days. *Who knew that poop could generate a sense of sweet fondness?* Eventually, our approach to those diaper changes became more like a team of Hazmat workers shrouded in contamination suits who were coming to save the world from the digestive wrath of a baby filled with radioactive waste. Amy thrived as a mother from the start. She is still the most naturally nurturing mom I have ever seen. She is the third generation of maternal excellence in her family. Deborah, Amy's mom, received that gift from her mother, Bonnie, and they passed it down to Amy. Alicia, now an adult, has the same anointing with children. It's an awesome sight to behold for me personally because my own mother struggled in the art of motherhood. Newborn Alicia immediately became the delight of our family. We still lived next door to the church, and I remember easy days with Alicia and me walking the parking lot with her safely nestled in a little vest against my chest. I would pray over her, try to sing over her, and then do all the goofy stuff that dads typically do with their little ones. When she was able to walk, she became an instant handful. Alicia was full of wonder and curiosity. She inspected things, loved to hold things, and run with those things. Her curiosity was beyond the norm that I had seen in other children. Many nights, Amy would collapse in bed after having chased after her daughter all day. My favorite daughter-daddy times with her would be within her gigantic play area in our oversized den in the parsonage next to the church. That area was filled with more toys than we could handle. Alicia and I would spend an hour or so every evening playing with the brightly colored, noisy, and fun toys that her grandparents and great aunts bought her. She also loved the park and the swings and anything that involved a stimulation to her senses. When I looked at her, there were times when I would just start crying with an admixture of joy and gratitude for God's grace to me. Alicia was a daily reminder that God had redeemed me from my dysfunctional childhood and subsequent years of darkness. This little girl was like a kiss from Heaven on my soul.

She still is.

Young parents, please know that when I tell you that your children's lives will rush past you quickly, I am not simply rehearsing words that all parents tend to say as their children get older. I really mean it. My little girl became a five-year-old riding her bike in our front yard. Twenty minutes later, she entered into the ultra-glittery delightful preteen season. An hour and a half after the glitter was gone, Alicia was a maturing high schooler who served underneath her teacher as the assistant director of her school's chorus. She walked the aisle in a red cap and gown after graduating with honors earning a 4.2 GPA. I blinked and Alicia was a legal voter, and then a vocational nanny and piano teacher. One day, some man will come and take her away to begin their married lives together. *That lucky sucker, whoever he is, better keep my little girl nearby her mother and me!* In all seriousness, if I could do it all over again, I would gladly strap her in that little baby-carrying vest and tote her around more frequently. I would stay in her playpen with her for two hours each evening instead of one. I would change her diapers with a little bit more gratitude for the privilege. I would work doubly hard at convincing her how precious she is and how loved she is by her daddy. Thankfully, my dreams for Alicia's future carry far more weight than do the regrets of my missed opportunities with her in the past. My daughter began as such a treasure. That treasure is far greater to me now than it was at the beginning.

If Alicia was my child of *wonder*, her brother, Landon, born five years after her, would be my child of *thunder*. Completely different from his sister, and equally loved, Landon would burst onto the scene of our family in June of 2005. Having a little parental experience under my belt, I approached the news of my son coming into the world a little differently than I did as a rookie dad. Firstly, Landon was a bit of an unexpected blessing. Amy and I were not sure when we would have children after Alicia. We took precautions so as not to conceive before we thought we were ready for baby number two. **How many of you have learned that, when God is not welcomed to rule, He will overrule?** Birth control was no match for the providence of God, and the exciting news of a baby boy on the way both humbled and thrilled me. I was ecstatic to learn that God was giving us a boy. At that time, there were nine other couples in the church expecting children, and all of them turned out to be baby boys except for one lone little girl. It looked like God was amassing an army of boys, and the church was abuzz for a while with all of the simultaneous conceptions taking place. Amy brought our son into the world through another tough, long labor. We took him home a few days later to begin our life as a family of four. Things felt complete for us when Landon arrived. I so wanted him to become a greater man than his father was, and I prayed that over him constantly until he was about nine years old. When I looked at his little face, I saw destiny. Landon is taller than me now, and when I look up into his face, I still see destiny. God is writing a story with my boy. I could not be prouder of him. He is a feeler who intuits the hearts of others much like his mother naturally does. The Father placed a relaxed spirit in Landon that I would have to take medication to have at work in my life. After the most painful season in our family's life, Landon emerged as God's chosen instrument of laughter and levity to us. When I get still and pray for him nowadays, I am filled with a certainty that the seeds planted in his heart by the Father will bring forth an orchard that will fill many people with multiple delicious fruits. I so love my son.

Very soon after we found our new rhythm as an enlarged family unit, we were alarmed with something for which we were completely unprepared. One afternoon, I received an urgent call at the church from Amy. She was obviously upset and relayed to me that, while she was changing Landon's diaper, **he had seized up** on the changing table. It only lasted a few moments, but it had terrified my sweet wife. Characteristically, I took the rational approach and talked her through the moment, asking questions, and making mental notes. She called her doctor and he encouraged us to take Landon in to be seen by a physician. It was maddening for us as parents, but all the tests came back normal, and there was nothing that the doctors could tell us unless they actually had him attached to their equipment while he was seizing. As far as they could tell, there was nothing wrong with our baby boy. We took him home and prayed over him, watching him constantly and wondering if it would happen again. He was not yet three months old.

It did, indeed, happen again a couple of evenings later while I was home. Few things are as troubling to a parent's heart than watching a child go through any type of physical trauma. As Amy had laid him down for another diaper change, he seized again, his little arms going rigid, his eyes wide open, and his tiny fists clenching. He came out of the episode quickly, but we knew something was just not right. Again, when we took him to the physician, there was nothing they could tell us. It is likely that they viewed us as paranoid parents who were merely being overprotective. This pattern continued off and on for a few more weeks with two or three more episodes that looked like seizures. We decided to take him to a prominent children's hospital in Atlanta and admit him for observation until we got some clear answers about what was happening to our son. Landon was right around four months old when he and Amy spent a long, dark week in that hospital. I was driving back and forth to be with them and then to go home and take care of Alicia after she came home from kindergarten each day. The amazing hospital staff ran unending tests on him, attaching him to machines with long technical names. Eventually, they experienced the occurrences of him seizing up while he was actually being monitored by their equipment. When they told us that these were not episodes connected to any sort of abnormal neurological activity, we were caught between deep relief and utter confusion. In essence, they told us that our baby boy *was not having seizures*. It looked like seizures, they told us, but his brain activity was normal at all times. The low point for me was when they told us that he would need to undergo a spinal tap to rule out viral possibilities. Amy is a warrior mom, but that was the moment she looked at me and let me know that I would be the parent who stood by Landon during that intense spine tapping procedure. I was more than willing to do this for her and our boy, but it was an awful moment when I held him to my chest as they swaddled him with a special garment that left an opening over his spinal column. I watched them insert the needle in his back as he was strapped belly down on the table. He screamed and screamed and screamed some more...*loudly*. I could see his eyes, wide open and staring at me, seemingly saying to me, "Come help me, daddy!" What he could not know is that we were all seeking to help him in those moments. Yet, what he needed

101

right then required him to be immobilized, without comfort, and forced to accept the pain of the needle that drew out the fluid from his tiny spine. I had never felt more inadequate as a Christian. Landon was not the only one who felt immobilized. **God had brought me to a place where I had nothing to offer.** If before I had regarded myself as a Superman, I was now fully aware that I was standing in a hospital lab full of Kryptonite.

Amy spent a full week in that hospital. She was alone at night, filled with mercy for her son who was struggling. I might have endured a moment of feeling helpless when he went through the spinal tap, but Amy never left the hospital for that full week. She had seven days of feeling her own powerlessness. Something was birthed in her heart that week while I was back home in Lawrenceville tending to Alicia. Those long nights in a hospital room might as well have been a boot camp for her soul. Amy came home *different* when the week concluded. **It would not be the last time that the Father visited my wife in private, profound ways while she was alone in a hospital room.** I will tell you more about that later.

When the week came to an end, and there were still zero answers about what was happening to Landon, we were told a long list of what was *not* wrong with him. According to the medical staff, our boy was perfectly healthy. In fact, he was the healthiest baby in their hospital. On the day of his discharge, the doctor told us that he likely had some form of intense acid reflux. They concluded that, when we laid him down for a diaper change, the acid came up from his stomach and into his esophagus, causing intense pain at which he would seize. It sounded more like an educated guess than anything else, but they had done all that they could, and we were finally free to go home. We left with Landon to travel home that evening, and all we really knew to do for him was pray. I fasted over his medical concerns, asking God for wisdom about what to do next. Amy mothered the boy with a fierce protectiveness. We laid our hands on him (yes, Baptists do that too), and prayed to the Lord to set him free from whatever it was that was happening to him. We were desperate for answers, but God never did clarify for us what the medical cause was for the seizure-like episodes.

We never did get the official answers. God did, however, completely deliver Landon from whatever had been happening to him. The seizing never recurred. Everything disappeared off the radar, and after hell week for Amy in the hospital with him, our son never again experienced any of the episodes that terrorized us for nearly two months. **He was healed, freed, and delivered.** If you ask Amy and me today what we believe the cause of the episodes was, we will tell you that we are both convinced that the enemy was trying to kill our son. If that makes us sound like fanatics to you, we can live with it. The best pediatric medical professionals in the Southeast watched Landon for a week, ran every possible test on him, witnessed what was happening with his little body…and had no medical answers other than a guess about it possibly being acid reflux. In the end, they offered us a very expensive, sincere, and sympathetic shrug.

When the natural medical explanations are ruled out for an affliction, we must consider *the supernatural.* The devil is real, and he is still an evil thief who steals, kills, and destroys whenever he is able. We called out to God on behalf of our son. We laid our hands upon his little body and declared him to be healed, freed, and delivered. We prayed, wept, and fasted. When we brought him home, all of the unexplained activity in his body ceased. Everything went back to a long-desired, long-absent normal. After a month of no new episodes, we turned the page and quit watching for the *bad stuff* to return. Our son was home, safe, and healthy. Life resumed and new chapters began to be written for Amy, Alicia, Landon, and me.

I so love my children. Those early days were a montage of mistakes, miscues, and mishaps by me as a dad. The Father was making me learn how to become a father. I was not an insta-dad who understood what his children needed. I had to figure it out as I go. God knew the best way to begin that work was to send me a daughter first, and a son next. Not just any daughter…Alicia. My daughter. Not just any son…Landon. My son. Along with their mother, God has used Alicia and Landon to teach me the depth of His own unconditional love for His children. I learned His heart toward me by receiving one for my own children. More times than I can count, I

103

have felt like Landon must have felt when he lay on that table, immobilized, frightened, and wondering why he was not being rescued. Looking back, I see clearly that my Father was working on levels that I could not comprehend. The pains, the loss of power, and the confusion were all occurring as God was working deeply in me for my own good. Landon looked like he wanted me to rescue him from all the bad stuff that day in the hospital. He could not have fathomed that it was all for his good. **I have learned that when God does not prevent the pain and remove the trouble, it does not diminish His goodness as my Father.** By faith, I understand that *there is so much that I cannot understand* in those moments. So, I wait. I trust. I believe that He is going to produce something glorious from the needling, the pains and the pressures. I received much of that understanding by experiencing what it means to love two children of my own. I want only their good – all the time.

Though I possess a ministerial graduate degree, marriage and parenthood have imparted far more understanding about the Father than any class, research paper, or thesis ever did. Almost as a sign and a wonder sent from Heaven, as my children began to grow up together, all of our lives would begin to change as God more precisely brought us onto the path that He had prepared for us. Both of our children would be acutely shaped by what would continue to find us in the early years of their lives. They do not currently understand how strong in the Spirit the Father has made them. They have had to be overcomers for most of their lives. I do not only love Alicia and Landon, but I also admire them. They are beautiful people. I am so blessed to be their father.

About five years after Landon's health battles, our gloriously good Father would entrust to all four of us Lyles a testing for which we could have never been prepared. Assumptions about our futures would be erased. The fairytale forecast of what it means to follow Jesus in faith would be replaced with a jagged reality that was anything but a fairytale. The darkest clouds for our family had not arrived yet. The threat of a greater storm was looming, but we were given no forecast nor warning. As a family, we would all soon be figuring it out as we went.

CHAPTER 17

An Intermission to Set the Stage

"This people honors Me with their lips, but their heart is far from Me;
in vain do they worship Me, teaching as doctrines the commandments of men."
– Matthew 15:8-9

IN THE NEXT CHAPTER, I will tell of the day where God radically overhauled me on the inside with what I call a *Holy Spirit ambush* in my office at the church. Nothing would be the same after that week for me, my family, or the flock I was leading. Before I share that account, I need to make sure the context for that dramatic occasion is fully understood by all of those reading.

Both of my children were involved in drama and theater classes during their school-age years. These low-budget performances were always a delight to us as their parents, as Alicia and Landon both had some natural skill for singing and acting that got better as they got older. At those middle-school and high-school performances, there is usually an intermission at the midway point of the play where some of the students will rush around to set the stage for whatever the next scene is going to be. You can hear them moving props around, taking down backdrops, and rolling in new staging behind the curtain. In my mind, I used to try and picture what it would look like before they finally raised the curtain to begin the second half of the production. Often, the newly visible setting for the stage immediately pointed toward what would be acted out next. *So, this is a good point for me to do the literary equivalent of that same type of stage setting.*

There was a firmly entrenched background for all that I was believing and doing during the early years of my walk with Jesus. I need to step back in time a little bit from where we left off in the previous chapter to provide some extremely important context for the atmosphere surrounding

Amy's and my entire married life and ministry life up to that point. To be perfectly accurate, this atmospheric reality lingered with us from all the way up through Alicia's birth and up to right around the time that Landon began first grade. During those years, God was working intentionally in my heart and also in Amy's heart concerning the deep need for us to experience freedom from the oppressive smog of man's religion that seemed to be everywhere we went in ministry opportunities and Christian events. Something begins to burrow down in a parent's heart when the things that the parents have learned to live with are now contextualizing the spiritual atmosphere in which their children are going to be raised. I am speaking specifically of various forms of *the spirit of religion*, specifically, denominational expectations in our church which resulted in some fairly frequent legalism. **My great concern became that I might advance in knowing the Word of God without learning the voice of God. I feared the possibility of gaining knowledge about Him but losing intimacy with Him.** I began to long even more for the Holy Spirit's presence and activity in my own heart. I had worked hard to exterminate this religious leaven of legalism from my own heart, our home life, and the church that I was helping lead. Because I refused to rule as a pastoral dictator, who would unilaterally change whatever he desired in order to suit his own personal preferences, there were still some religiously toned issues that seemed to lurk around the church, serving to occasionally grieve and provoke me in my spirit. There was this mildew of old religion in our church that badly needed the bleach of Gospel liberation. I would eventually tackle this issue head on beginning in my first month of becoming the Senior Pastor in 2002. Before that season arrived, however, the intentional pursuit of the Lord found me. He had determined to free me completely from the last links in my stubborn chains of fundamentalist, denominationally unquestionable religion.

When Alicia was close to turning two years old, we were getting ready to move from the parsonage into a house about fifteen minutes north of the church. My mother-in-law, Deborah, came to see her daughter and granddaughter one day, and she was at the house when I crossed the parking lot to come home from the office. Casually, she handed me a boxed set of sermons on cassette tapes from Charles Swindoll. Still conditioned by my fundamentalist Baptist ways, I remember saying to her rather gruffly, *"Charles Swindoll? Isn't he one of those liberal Christians?"* I wish I could go back in time and punch my thirty-one-year-old self in the face for being so rude and foolish to that godly woman. Deborah simply lowered her eyes and said gently, "Well, he has been a blessing to me, and I thought you might like to hear these messages." She set the box of tapes on the table and went back to the other room where there was a loving daughter and delightful granddaughter awaiting her. I felt like a jerk. That feeling was not misguided. The next day, because I so respected Deborah's walk with Jesus, I popped in the first cassette from that sermon series and began to listen. Surprisingly, I enjoyed this man who was not a part of my denominational tribe. He spoke of grace, truth, love, and freedom with an anointed eloquence that beckoned me to listen to the next message. The second sermon had the same inviting quality to it, and before I left the office that day, I had listened to the first six messages in Dr. Swindoll's series. What was it that made me respond so *hungrily* to this man's preaching? I could not have told you at the time, but now I recognize that **the Holy Spirit was stirring within me as God's Word was being accurately taught in the absence of man's religion and traditions**. There were no pastoral threats. No manipulation was being released by the preacher. He did not come off as the all-knowing boss of his congregation. He was not compromising anything from the Bible as he taught in wisdom and gentleness; even his rebukes felt like an invitation to press in closer to Jesus. On top of everything, I saw that he was actually pastoring his flock via the scriptures. He was preaching *for* the congregation for their good, not *at them* for getting his point across. The day before, I had basically rebuked my devoted mother-in-law for handing me these presumably spiritually soiled cassettes from some liberal pastor from California, but now I was devouring them as the greatest spiritual delicacy I had ever sunk my teeth into! Nobody I had ever heard had impacted me as this man did with his exposition of the scriptures. Where had he been my whole Christian life? Before too long, I had ordered nearly everything that Charles Swindoll ever made available on cassette. Through the preached

Word by Charles Swindoll, God was rewiring my entire mindset concerning the Kingdom, grace, compassion, kindness, patience, and the heart of the Father. It seemed that, for the very first time, I was seeing the fruit of the Holy Spirit on full display. I could understand righteousness apart from regulations for the first time in my life as a Jesus follower. Fear-based behavioral modification no longer lived inside of me. The Holy Spirit was delivering me from the legalism in my own heart, and I was breathing in fresh spiritual air every day. Glory to God…I was getting free!

Now, there was a ton of repenting going on in this particular season of my life — truthfully, nearly every single day. God was exposing my own heart to me and was bringing me to deeper levels of confession. I grieved at all of the legalism and judgmentalism that had been home in my heart for nearly my entire Christian experience. While I was still serving in a denominational paradigm that exalted external standards and longstanding traditions, inwardly and privately, I was experiencing some intense personal transformation. By the way, the only person I was sharing this with was Amy. I dared not tell my pastor or anyone else at the church. It was a breathtakingly spectacular season for me privately, but I felt isolated at our church, as I continued to serve as the Associate Pastor. After Pastor Jack resigned in the summer of 2002, the church approved me to replace him in the autumn of that same year. The freedom from legalism that was churning within me now had an outlet *to flow out from me*. I knew that there would need to be much prayer and wisdom for me to discern from God how to enter into a ministry of reformation at the church. I learned to wait on the Lord and to lead at the pace that he was setting. **Reformation of man-oriented traditional churches is not for the faint of heart.** The people I pastored loved Jesus and were earnest believers for the most part. Yet, these same precious people had been spiritually reared to believe a certain way, and much of what we had all been taught had its root system in man's traditions more so than God's written Word.

Slowly, I began to introduce freedom from certain legalistic mandates within our church. We removed things like dress codes for men, women, and children. I preached biblical modesty from the pulpit while allowing for the revelation that women could wear pants and not be grieving the Holy Spirit by doing so. We addressed generational stylistic controls of our music program by adding modern choruses to traditional hymns. I really rolled the dice when I allowed for our children's ministry leaders to use a curriculum that was not from the King James translation of the scriptures. With each and every change, there was at least a little pushback. We lost our biggest financial contributor when I refused to mandate from the pulpit that the women had to start wearing only skirts and dresses again. He pronounced *anathema* on the church and left hurt and angry. Some dear people who could not endure the stylistic changes in the music left too. These things seem so puny and silly now, but at that time, it was nothing short of the beginnings of the growing pains which always accompany the ministry of reformation within a church. When God initiates a heart, a family, a church, or a denomination to be reformed, there will be plenty of dust that flies. It is guaranteed that people will leave. Leaders will be misunderstood, mistreated, and misrepresented by some of those who leave. Courageous continuance must be retained by those leaders. I had to learn all of this the hard way because I had never met anyone who had done what I was being led to do by God. I was figuring it out on the go. **Leaders who are addicted to people's approval will not survive the work of a reformer.** As I began repenting before God privately for the past legalistic way I had represented Him to others, there was no way I could allow these same issues to be further galvanized and perpetuated in our church family.

Things were dramatically changing at the church, and lots of questions were finding me from among the flock every week. Most, in the church family, were coming alive and were thrilled with the introduction of the concept of biblical liberty. Their own sacred cows had not been tipped, so they were pleased with the new freedom and sense of God's presence powerfully coming to us through the changes we were making. It was the beginning of a long and intense season of pursuing the Lord in new ways. I would do many things differently if I had the chance to go back and do the whole process over again, **but I would never choose not to do it.** While I made many rookie mistakes, I do not regret those early days as a pastor. The thrill of obeying God in the risky mission He had entrusted to me as a young leader brought deep satisfaction to my soul. While it felt like that season was a harvest of great things and profound reformation, I would see later on that this season truly was not a harvest time. It was just the start of a work that would last more than a decade longer.

In that season, we were just beginning to till up the ground. I was learning as I went that reforming the church requires that you dig deeply.

CHAPTER 18

The Day God Pounced

"As I began to speak, the Holy Spirit fell on them just as on us at the beginning. And I remembered the word of the Lord, how He said, 'John baptized with water, but you will be baptized with the Holy Spirit.' If then God gave the same gift to them as He gave to us when we believed in the Lord Jesus Christ, who was I that I could stand in God's way?"
– Acts 11:15-17

As a man whom God was delivering from legalism and dead tradition, I wanted to remain devotedly consistent in making sure I was still growing in my understanding of the Bible. To provide for my own spiritual growth, I continued a regimen of daily Bible reading and prayer. For me, both then and now, an intentional approach to prayer and study of the Scriptures has — never been about some religious checklist. I love God. I love God's Word. We receive revelation of His heart, His ways, and His works as we read His book of Kingdom truth. Though my own prayer life has gone through several measurable stages of evolution, I have always treasured the priceless privilege of crying out to a God who listens to me and answers back. In February of 2003, less than three full months after I was made Meadow Baptist's Senior Pastor, I took my place behind the large cherry-wood desk in my office at the church. I had my starched dress shirt buttoned to the top and my brightly colored power tie knotted just below my Adam's apple. Per the established manner of all pastors at Meadow, I dressed that way every day for work. It was not yet six in the morning when I began my formal time of prayer and study. My office desktop phone was on Do Not Disturb. My Bible was open on my desk. The Bible study software was open to the place where I had been studying the morning before. This was my favorite time of the day, and I was eager to sit down and let the Kingdom festivities begin.

In those days, I always prayed before I started my morning reading, so I bowed my head and begin to express my adoration of God. I searched my heart and confessed any sin that came to mind that had occurred since the last time I had talked with Him. As usual, within my normal prayer flow, I began to thank Him for Amy, Alicia (Landon was still a couple of years away at this point), the ministry He had entrusted to me, and whatever/whoever else was on my prayer list for that particular day. What happened next was definitely not on my agenda, nor was it written anywhere on my prayer list. Let me describe those moments to the best of my human ability. I intentionally have refused over the years to make this spiritual encounter anything other than what it was that day:

It was a full-scale, sovereignly initiated, Heaven-scheduled, unprecedented, unannounced ambush of my life by the third Person of the Godhead, none other than the **Holy Spirit**. Or, for people who prefer a more succinct description: *God pounced.*

Let me explain.

As I went a little further into my normal prayer routine, I remember beginning to feel tremendous joy swirling inside of me as I continued to give thanks to God for all that He had granted to me. My normal outward expression is not necessarily one of overflowing joy. It really never has been. Although I am passionate and expressive in my faith, *joyfully exuberant* is not a description that most people would immediately associate with me upon first impression. On this particular day, in a very short time, I was inwardly eclipsing any previous sense of joy I had ever experienced. I felt it moving in my whole body. Literally, I could feel the substance of joy in my limbs, my back, and my stomach. My prayers and thanksgiving quickly erupted into tearful praise. Thankfully, nobody else was in the office that early, so my volume increased as did my sense of God's presence in my office. Now, please remember that I had been a very committed Baptist boy for all eight-and-a-half years of my Christian life. I had only been to one Charismatic church service during that time, and it was a bit of a bust. Only once before in my childhood had I ever heard anyone speak in tongues, and quite honestly, it frightened me as a young boy. I had not specifically asked God for any particular gift of the Holy Spirit, although I had been praying for nearly a year for Him to give me all that He wanted for me. On that particular morning, as this volcanic joy began to move powerfully inside of me, my prayers in the English language became prayers in a language like I had never heard. Foreign sounds were coming out of my mouth during prayer. **For the first time in my life, I had just spoken in tongues.** No more than ten or fifteen syllables came out of me in that odd-sounding speech before I literally clamped both of my hands over my mouth. My denominational instinct intruded into this undefinable spiritual experience, and guilt and fear hit me as strongly as the joy had hit a few minutes earlier. I literally said out loud to God, *"I'm sorry, Lord."*

I want to be as clear as I can be. God had sovereignly bestowed upon me the gift of tongues in my office in February of 2003, just a few short months after I had been installed as the Senior Pastor of *Meadow Independent Fundamental Baptist Church*. I did not ask Him for this gift. I did not necessarily want this gift. I had not heard anyone speak in tongues except for the one occasion more than two decades earlier as a boy. What came out of my mouth that morning was an unsolicited manifestation of God the Spirit moving powerfully within me. Though it was a sovereignly bestowed gift, it also required my cooperation and faith for it to continue. As quickly as it had come, I shut it down because all my denominational, theological rearing had taught me that this was an invalid gift that disappeared from the Church near the end of the first century. I fancied myself an academic, not a Charismatic! We even had a man in our church at that time who wrote and personally printed a Gospel tract that attributed all modern use of tongues as being sourced in demonic activity! Dozens of those tracts were sitting in a wall-mounted rack just down the hall from the very office where I had just been ambushed from Heaven and found myself praying and praising God in tongues. After the awkward apology I offered to God, I remember sitting silently for a minute or two trying to process with my mind what had just occurred in my spirit. I composed myself and tentatively began praying again in English. With measured, deliberate sentences, I defaulted back to a normal mode of praying through a list. While my mind was birthing the prayers, I became aware that something else was happening at a parallel pace in my spirit. Again, large waves of joy washed over me, and within a minute or two, the second wave of unintelligible speech came out of my mouth. **Tongues 2.0 found me just minutes after I had wrestled with guilt about having encountered it the first time!** *What was happening to me? What was God doing?* While I could not explain the experience, I also could not deny the joy that was connected to it. Sadly, the cemented years of my denominational standards won the moment, and I literally got up out of my office and just abruptly decided that my prayer time was officially over. I did not tell a soul about what had happened that day.

The next day was akin to *wash, rinse, and repeat.* I entered my office early in the morning and approached my desk with my Bible, my Bible software, my journal, and my prayer list. By the way, there was also a gigantic elephant in the room that I was trying to ignore. I remember wondering if anything *weird* would happen again. I won't devote a lot of time and space to describing the experience on that second morning but suffice it to say that it followed the spiritual template from the day before. This time, I knew that what was happening was not wrong. I knew that no demon would want me to experience the love and joy of God in that way, nor could any demon counterfeit this sense of God's powerful presence. *It felt utterly holy.* I knew deep within me that it was God. It completely broke my theological grid, but I was convinced that the Holy Spirit had baptized me into a fullness of Himself that I had never known. **Tongues were real.** The gift of tongues was not a historical relic belonging to bygone eras of ancient church history. The Holy Spirit, in those two days in my office, sealed in me forever the conviction that He is a full-contact, sovereign God who disburses His *charismata* (spiritual gifts) to whom He wants, when He wants, and for the purposes He wants. By the way, all of that is clearly written in Scripture in **1ˢᵗ Corinthians 12:4-6**. Sadly, I have to confess that, although I knew that what had happened with me was genuine, I caved in to practical logic mixed in with the fear of man. In one of the most regrettable prayers I have ever offered, I told God that I did not want anything more of this gift in my life. I literally fumbled up some explanation to the Almighty that, as a new Baptist pastor, I could not be a tongue-talker. I explained to Omniscience that it would split the church and kill my ministry. I played the coward but called it prudence. I acted in unbelief and passed it off as wisdom. I quenched the Spirit by declining the furtherance of the flame of this gift in my life. **For about two more years, the gift of tongues never reappeared in me.** I would not be reintroduced to this gift that I now treasure until I was brought to a place of utter brokenness during a season where I came again to the end of my own strength. How I regret now that, when God offered me something glorious in those early days as a pastor, I said to Him, "No thank you."

Some of you will struggle with everything that I just shared. Believe me, I understand why. For those of you who do not believe in the validity of the gift of tongues, you may very well think that I simply had some uber-emotional experience that caused me to do something childish or silly. Maybe some of you even think that a demon got a hold of me that day, initiating some counterfeit experience to knock me off the straight and narrow. Others of you from more of a Charismatic background might question how in the world I could shut down a spiritual gift from God that is so precious to the Christian experience. You might also wonder why God would ambush me with a gift that I was not seeking, did not really want, and temporarily refused to use. Whatever your individual struggle might be with what I have shared, I just want you to know that you will receive zero judgment from me for wrestling with my testimony. I only want you to know that the story is true. I have put my name and my credibility on the line by sharing it, and **doing so has already cost me much with people,** but praying tongues has deepened me so much in — God. I would find out later that almost nobody receives the gift of tongues — in the manner I was given it. If I had to offer any attempt to explain why God might have chosen this sovereignly bestowing mode with me, I would only hazard the guess that He knew I would never ask it from Him for myself. Yet, He had clearly determined to give it to me. He gave me a tiny taste of the power of the Kingdom that was completely shut off from me due to my theological training and denominational traditions. At that time, even before my personal encounter, I already believed the gifts of the Holy Spirit were theoretically still available, but I never actually thought I needed any supernatural touch from God for myself. I was a Bibleman (and still am!). My confidence was in God's Word, and I never sensed any need for something beyond that. When God the Spirit sovereignly ambushed me in my office that day, *He gave me a taste to let me learn if I desired to receive the whole bite.*

May I say something to all of you who love Jesus and retain a strong commitment to the Word of God? Would you be willing to hazard a commitment to seeking God by asking Him to give you <u>everything</u> that is available for you in Christ? I do not want that to sound condescending. I actually believe it is a prayer we should all constantly be offering to the One who has purchased us with the blood of His Son. As a Christian who was theologically trained to not believe in the gifts of the Holy Spirit, it was actually my confidence in the unadulterated interpretation of the scriptures that eventually brought me to the firm conviction that there is not a single verse in the Bible that tells us that the gifts of the Holy Spirit have currently ceased. **Not a single verse.** I was a theological continuationist (one who believes in the present validity of the gifts of the Holy Spirit) for close to two years before I ever personally experienced a supernatural gift of the Spirit. My Bible told me the gifts were *available to me.* The Spirit made the gifts *actual in me.* Were it not for 1st Corinthians 13:8, there would actually not be any debate at all about whether or not these gifts of the Spirit have ceased. Ponder that the abundance of verses in Acts and 1st Corinthians which clearly reveal spiritual gifts to be active among all types of believers has all been explained away due to the tiny shadow that is cast by 1st Corinthians 13:8. That one verse is so easily interpreted properly by just taking an honest look at the verses which immediately follow it. The gifts of the Holy Spirit are active and available to you – *all of them!* We are actually commanded to desire the gifts in earnestness. Yet, so many of us have been told that they are not available. Many of us have been taught that anyone using them today is a counterfeit.

Would it not be just like Satan to create a doctrine that leaves us with the view that the gifts of the Holy Spirit that were so essential to the first century Church have never been available to any believer in the centuries which followed? If we cannot have God's supernatural gifting, then all we are left with is sound theological understanding, committed disciplines, human experience and ingenuity, and some form of Christian faith that is devoid of God's supernatural power. That strikes me as a teaching that would clearly evoke a hearty AMEN from Hell.

We need His power. We need His gifts. God is calling so many in this current generation to topple the altars of their denominational expectations and to bow afresh at the unfiltered truth of the Word. I hope that this chapter will serve to spark a hunger in some who are unable to continue to settle for the status quo, Western, post-enlightenment expression of Christianity. It was not just my home church that stood in need of a reformation of the Spirit. It is the great need of churches everywhere in God's Kingdom.

We need the Holy Spirit. We need everything that He has for us.

CHAPTER 19

The Hollowness of Success

*"But whatever gain I had, I counted as loss for the sake of Christ. Indeed,
I count everything as loss because of the surpassing worth of knowing
Christ Jesus my Lord. For His sake I have suffered the loss of
all things and count them as rubbish, in order that I may gain Christ."*
– Philippians 3:7-8

AFTER MY ENCOUNTER WITH THE Holy Spirit in my office, I entered into a four-year season of working diligently to lead our church family into an unwavering commitment to align fully with God's truth in both our identity and our mission. My assignment from heaven during that season was to lead our church family to become people of confidence in *the veracity of the Bible*. I failed to note the inconsistency of my own unwillingness to personally walk in the revelation of the power of the Holy Spirit which I had experienced. I had made my regrettable decision not to pursue anything further in the way of supernatural encounter with Him. Ever the pragmatist, I chose to focus on jettisoning the unbiblical traditions that were constricting Meadow Baptist from walking in the freedom of God's written Word. I preached on the sovereignty of God, the glories of His goodness, His infinite worth, and His eternal Lordship. I created a leadership team with whom I could run hard and fast, and we became great friends and brothers. The church was now trending younger, and the older generation was very happy, at that time, due to the heavy theological emphasis that had emerged in who we were, what was being preached, and all that we sang together when we gathered. People were being saved and baptized, and it was really an enjoyable season. Frankly, it was pretty much what most young pastors long for in the ministries that have been entrusted to them. The church was booming, and very soon we were running out of space. There were certainly some growing pains, but I handled those issues quickly and decisively, not allowing for any type of disgruntledness to spread in the flock. Looking back on that particular season now, I would simply say that it was a time wherein everything I put my hand to turned to gold. *Everything* worked. God, in spite of my unwillingness to operate any further in the gifts of the Holy Spirit, was blessing me in ministry. He was allowing me to operate in my own strength in many areas while I continued to conveniently avoid the issue of the gifts of the Holy Spirit. Very soon, I would learn what happens to a person at the end of that isolating road whereupon he or she is saying no to God's supernatural powers.

When the time came that we began discussing the need to relocate to a larger facility to accommodate the growing number of people who were coming, I felt like I had accomplished something significant in the Kingdom. I do not remember feeling proud about any of it. *I felt satisfied.* I felt as if I had done something that would please my Heavenly Father. For the first time in my life, I could measure some success. Goals were made, goals were reached, results were good, and ministry seemed like something for which I was made. After a diligent process, the church family agreed to sell our current facility and relocate about ten minutes away to a much larger, newer, and nicer facility on thirteen acres in Lawrenceville. Our bank gladly worked with us, and we established a bridge loan on our current property and went ahead and purchased the new building. It was June of 2008, and we signed on the dotted line and began to prepare to move. Yes, we now had a six-million-dollar loan on the new property, but our current property would easily and quickly sell for that amount, and we would be debt free before the end of the year after the right buyer came to purchase our former location.

Oh, by the way, in case you were unaware, **the real estate market crashed in the fall of 2008**, just a few months after we listed our property for sale. Our former location became one of the countless real estate transactions that refused to budge. What should have been a quick, profitable sale ended up being a two-year journey of futility. The bridge loan between the new and the old property was not paid off in weeks or months. That piece of real estate sat unsold for nearly *two years*. Interest accrued and the monthly payments were putting a stranglehold on the church finances. Behind the scenes, I was inwardly dying. Though the church was still growing, and the weekly ministries were well-attended, the financial situation was looking bleak. From 2003 to mid-2008, everything I touched was gold. Beginning in late 2008, everything I touched turned to trouble. Nothing worked. My weekly staff meetings turned into pathetic times of me communicating my stresses and fears to my co-laborers. No longer was I able to be satisfied with ministry success. Those days had vanished, and I was inwardly dying. God had allowed me to soar to the heights of where my own leadership skills, spiritual disciplines, careful planning, team building, and vision would take me.

Then He let me crash and burn into a steaming pile of ministry manure.

It was the wisest, most merciful thing that Abba could have done for me at that time. It broke me. More precisely, it began the breaking of me. So much more happened during that long season between 2008 and 2014. Yes, it took six full years of God's proactive disciplining of me for me to reach a fullness of surrender to Him that would be necessary for me to step into all that He had prepared for me. Later, I would label this season as **the consecration of my crushing.** While there was one singular event that would define the years of my crushing (I will devote an entire chapter to this lone event), I will list some others as I finish this chapter.

For anyone reading who is involved in any type of ministry, whether vocational or volunteer, you should know that ministry costs you and occasionally hurts you deeply. It exposes your weaknesses and insecurities. Don't bother bringing your fig leaves into ministry because you will eventually have to drop them. This is part of the process by which God never allows us to trust in the ministry as being essential to our identity. We simply cannot tie any significant portion of our identity to our ministries. He does not desire for us to fall into the error of Martha who was so preoccupied with serving Jesus that she missed an opportunity to sit at His glorious feet with her sister, Mary, and simply *be with Jesus* **(see Luke 10:38-42).** Ministry for Jesus is to flow from intimacy and identity in Jesus. If that equation ever gets upside down in our lives, God will purposefully frustrate our ministry. Sometimes He will shut that ministry down because He does not actually need it. **He wants you more than He wants your activities for Him.** In my own case, I was serving Him sincerely, innocently, and diligently. I really did think I was doing it rightly. It had worked brilliantly for so many years, but those years had ended, and a new season of frustration, fear, and futility had arisen. Here is what some of that season of consecration via crushing looked like for me:

- I switched Bible translations from the King James Version and lost multiple families who held the conviction that any other translation of God's Word was sinful. I became known as the corrupt and compromised Independent Baptist pastor who abandoned the pillar of all our essential traditions when I no longer used the KJV to preach.

- A staff member began to lead his volunteer team and the assigned ministry group in a direction different from the rest of what was happening at the church. When confronted, he refused to comply with leadership. He resigned angrily and left the church in such a way that relationships were irreparably harmed, and my own reputation was ruined with many over the division. His life also fell apart. It was a time of brokenheartedness for both of us. Most of all, I mourned the loss of my friend.

- The church continued to decline financially. Even when the former property sold, it was for half of the original lowest appraisal. We were saddled with over four million dollars of debt. This process knocked the wind out of me.

- A dear friend who was so pivotal in the early days of my Christian life became an influential leader in our church, and eventually, he stealthily led about a dozen younger couples out of our church due to my departure from traditions that he personally held dearly. It felt like another layer of betrayal and rejection.

- My wife endured hostility from some of the women in the church whose husbands had issues with my leadership. I was made for war.

121

Before this season, Amy was not. When my sweet wife became the target of ungodly gossip and slander from women, the weight became increasingly difficult to bear as her husband.

- The water main to our building erupted underneath the floor in our lobby. This happened sometime on a Saturday, and we were not there to discover it until Sunday morning, a few hours before service was to begin. The entire downstairs, our children's ministry area, was flooded and a 15 × 15 foot area right in the middle of our main lobby had to be completely dug out to repair the break. The damage took nearly two months to fully fix and cost quite a sum of money that the church did not have to spare.

- I was accused by a man in the church of making an absurd amount of money as my salary. He told people that he had proof that I was making more than three times my actual salary. I had actually not taken a personal raise for more than eight years at that point, but he would hear none of it. Eventually, I offered him a full look at my tax returns and W2's to show him that he was wrong. He refused to open the large, legal envelope with my financial documents, he stuck to his story, and he continued to spread his lies before leaving the church. My reputation had taken another heavy blow. Others also left with him over the issue. None of them asked for an opportunity to hear from me or view my financials.

- More difficult than anything else, the Lord had gone pretty much silent on me during these days. He heard me crying every day to Him for relief. No relief came. Only *more* crushing. **God was not punishing me.** He was testing the level of my trust, and I was daily struggling to pass that test.

So, this was the big lesson I learned during that long and maddening season: **success is overrated**. Ministry success is even more overrated. I had accomplished what many pastors never get to see. Outwardly, I appeared to others as a successful minister. In just five years, I had grown a church to the point where we had to relocate to larger facilities. I founded a separate television and media ministry which was doing some fruitful work both in

America and overseas via missions. I had been used by God to reform a traditional church into a biblically defined church. Yes, I had swum with the current of ministry achievements... and I ended up gagging on and nearly drowning in those waters of success. I definitely would have drowned in them had it not been for a merciful Father who refused to let me continue to prosper without Him near and center. I wrote earlier that, amid all the things listed above and many more that I chose not to write, there was one singular event that awakened me and Amy to the depths of faith which God had appointed to us. Let me share that part of the story next.

SECTION 5
WITH HIM

CHAPTER 20
Collision: When the Unforeseen Crashes In

"Behold, I go forward, but He is not there, and backward, but I do not perceive Him;
on the left hand when He is working, I do not behold Him;
He turns to the right hand, but I do not see Him. But He knows the way that I take;
when He has tried me, I shall come out as gold."
– Job 23:8-10

ALICIA WAS SOON TO TURN eleven and Landon would be six in a week. The date was June 16, 2011, and it happened to be my forty-first birthday. I came home from work to a house occupied by my three precious ones, plus my mother-in-law and father-in-law. Danny and Deborah were a constant fixture in our lives, and they deeply loved their grandchildren. Amy and Deborah got into Amy's car to go get some birthday dinner and my cake from a shopping area a couple of miles from our home. It was highly unusual for Alicia not to be jumping into the mix when both her mother and grandmother were going somewhere together. For some reason, on this particular day, she declined to get in the car with them and chose instead to hang out with me, her little brother, and her grandfather. That was nothing short of the providence of God as we would soon see.

After an hour had passed without them returning home with the cake and food, I began to wonder what was going on. We were having fun goofing around, but in the back of my mind, I recognized that my internal clock was telling me that Amy should have been back by now. My phone rang, but it was a number I did not recognize so I chose not to pick up. About fifteen minutes later, I walked out of the den, where Alicia and Landon were enjoying some high-volume fun with Danny, and I stepped onto the front porch to call Amy to see what was taking so long. As I opened my phone, I saw that there was a voicemail notification from the phone number I did not recognize from earlier. I hit the play button and heard a man's voice informing me that he was a witness to an auto collision involving my wife. Apparently, immediately after the collision, Amy had been screaming out for someone to call her husband and had given this bystander my phone number before she lost consciousness. I immediately called the man back and learned that he had witnessed a larger vehicle cross the center line at full speed and crash headlong into Amy's little car which was traveling at full speed from the opposite direction. He told me that there was no way for me to get to the scene because traffic was stopped in both directions. Eventually, he handed the phone to an officer on the scene who let me know that I should meet them at the hospital that was fifteen minutes from my house. **The wreck had actually occurred nearly an hour before I got the man on the phone.** Deborah had been cut out of Amy's vehicle and was already in transport to the hospital. Amy was pinned tightly in the vehicle, and they were having much more difficulty getting her out.

Fewer things in my life have been more difficult than walking back inside and needing to figure out how to explain to my father-in-law and children what had happened. With Danny, I needed to be clear and detailed as it was his wife that was in trouble. With my children, I needed to be calm and reassuring, as it was their mommy who was hurt. This moment was way beyond my skill set as a father. I don't even remember what I said, but I communicated to my father-in-law privately and the children separately about the wreck. Danny left immediately to go and be with Deborah at the hospital. I had to call some dear friends, an older couple that was very close to our family, to come to my house and take my kids with them so I could leave to be with Amy. Looking back, I can only imagine the fear and dread in the young hearts of my daughter and son. Their mommy and grandmother were hurt and being taken to the hospital. Their daddy had to leave them and go to be with their mommy. They were left without full explanations. I was left without choices. By the time I got to the local hospital, I learned that Amy had been taken to a different hospital in downtown Atlanta, over two hours in drive time due to traffic. When I was still fifteen minutes from the correct hospital, waiting for vehicles ahead of me to move forward in bumper to bumper traffic, an ambulance came up behind me in full lights-and-sirens mode. *I wondered if it could possibly be my wife whom they were transporting in that emergency vehicle. Surely, she was already being cared for down at the hospital. Surely, she was not actually behind me.* It turned out that it was, indeed, Amy in that ambulance. So mangled was her car that it took a couple of hours to cut her free from the vehicle. That is why she was behind me instead of awaiting me at Atlanta Medical Center. My sweet, beautiful wife had been stuck in a mangled car in Georgia's summer heat for over two hours with injuries that would prove to be horrific.

This was the worst moment of our lives together…and we were not actually together yet. Again, I found myself in that frighteningly familiar place where life was happening to me…and I did not have a voice in how any of it would play out. Powerlessness was my reality again. Here was yet another instance where God was putting on full display that I was severely limited. I did not like it at all. No gifting, no strength, no theology, no success, no intellect – nothing – could fix what had happened that day. My wife, who was my best friend, was hurt and I was stuck in traffic without even the ability to get to her. *We were supposed to be home eating birthday cake.* Instead, we were faced with life and death staring us down and seemingly… tauntingly… asking us if there was anything we would like to say.

I had nothing. It felt like the worst of dreams.

Like Job, in the words at the beginning of this chapter, I lost my sense of God being present and active. I could not find Him. I was alone in my truck in standstill Atlanta traffic while my wife was injured somewhere in the city. My precious mother-in-law was somewhere else in a critical state. My children were without a mommy to hug them or a daddy to protect or reassure them. I began to weep in my truck just wanting my Father to move the cars out of my way so I could get to Amy. Hot tears of frustration streamed down my cheeks as I secretly wondered if Amy would be alive when I got there.

God was silent. God was still. God did not make the bad go away.

But, not for a second, did I feel that God was not still good.

I could not feel His presence, but I knew that my faithful Father had not abandoned me. *He was engaged.* He was with Amy. He was with Deborah and Danny. He was with Alicia and Landon. My emotions sensed His seeming absence, but my faith was resting in His undiluted goodness. I waited on Him as the traffic began to move. When I finally was able to park and enter the emergency room, the Great Comforter was present, and I knew that He was holding my hand.

It's a good thing that He was because what awaited me in that ER nearly took my feet out from under me.

CHAPTER 21

Amy and Jeff, Meet Your New Normal

"Do not boast about tomorrow, for you do not know what a day may bring."
- Proverbs 27:1

THEY HAD CUT OFF ALL her clothes. Her arms were black and blue and swollen. Her torso was deeply bruised. It was almost impossible for me to look at her right ankle. It was turned at a ghastly angle, even though the physicians had clearly taken strides to stabilize it. Her clothes were bloodied and laying on the floor. She had a seatbelt or airbag burn across her chest which was naked and exposed. I remember thinking that my modest wife would not want all these people seeing her exposed. It's funny how the mind works sometimes. With the excruciating pain she was in and the catastrophic injuries she had incurred, the last thing Amy was worried about was strangers seeing her chest. I was supposed to do a wedding rehearsal for our friends, Jill and Jeff, the next night and the wedding the following day. I actually remember wondering if I could leave the hospital to get the wedding done once they stabilized Amy. That is how far from reality I was operating having no real clue that Amy was not merely dealing with a busted ankle. We would find out later that she came close to death in that car that day.

Everything was changing for us.

The doctors gave me about a five-minute update and prognosis. They were going to be doing Amy's first surgery immediately to try and save her lower leg. The doctor was candid with me and told me that they were not optimistic about her being able to keep it. Her ribs were all broken. She had a broken hand, arm, elbow, and fingers. Her sternum was cracked. The leg was their most urgent concern. Apparently, when they cut her out, her ankle was basically hanging off the rest of her leg by a mangled mess of internal ligaments, tendons, and skin. The doctor mentioned that they were calling in a very skilled orthopedic surgeon who was in another wing of the hospital. It turns out that this particular doctor was the most skilled orthopedic trauma surgeon in the nation at that time. He just happened to be in the hospital that day when he was not actually scheduled for any surgeries. Amy just happened to get rerouted to Atlanta Medical Center where he was working. This man may have been the only person in the state of Georgia who could potentially save Amy's leg. I kissed my wife's forehead and watched them take her back on a gurney to the operating room. About twelve hours later, I would finally see her again in her hospital room.

"It looked like a grenade went off in there. I was picking out bone fragments for over an hour, one-by-one." That is what Amy's surgeon told me. He said he could not say with any certainty that the surgery would prove successful. This guy was cool, calm, and collected. I could tell that he was deeply challenged by Amy's injuries and consequent surgical needs. When all was said and done, He basically left me with the answer, "Time will tell. I cannot make any promises about her future and that right leg."

The major thing I was feeling was relief. Amy would not die. If she lost her leg, I could live with that as long as I still had the love of my life to hold. The news my father-in-law received was not as hopeful. Deborah had been devastatingly wounded in the wreck. She was on life support. Her seatbelt harness in the car had snapped, and she had been violently tossed around the vehicle at impact. Amy remembers looking down as she went in and out of consciousness, and her mother was strewn across Amy's lap bleeding. The heartbreaking news would arrive early in the morning several days later when Deborah Samples slipped into the presence of the One she adored. My precious mother-in-law finished her race on earth, having never awakened after the initial impact of the collision. **Amy's mother, Danny's wife, my children's MaMa was now in Heaven.** Amy never knew that their moments of laughter and joy right before the man crashed his car into them were the final moments she would ever share on earth with her best friend and mother.

For the next month, Amy would endure several more surgeries, the rigors of learning how to sit, stand, and be transferred to a wheelchair. Both her arms were in casts. She literally only had her left leg as a functional limb for nearly two full months. We learned how to do life together as a couple experiencing a new way of living daily, navigating through her disabilities. When Amy finally came home, she stayed in a hospital bed in our den for another month while her body continued to heal. They had her on massive narcotics to deal with the intense pain. Fentanyl patches, Oxycodone, muscle relaxers, antibiotics for her wounds and anti-inflammatories were her daily reality. About a week after coming home, Amy unilaterally decided she did not want to be on the Fentanyl patches anymore. Under the care of a dear friend who was a pharmacist, Amy weaned herself cold turkey off of the patches. She literally refused to continue the heaviest of her pain medications from that point forward. She had been on those patches for over a month, and I watched her press through withdrawal for a solid thirty-six hours. Then it was done. *You know how she coped during her withdrawals?* She chewed two large tubs of bubble gum that I bought at Costco. God is amazing! So is my wife! Amy came off of massive doses of Fentanyl via nonstop bubble gum chewing wherein she released all of the tension and pains of narcotic withdrawal. Amy weaned herself off it completely. After that victory, she decided the Oxycodone was also robbing her of peace and a sense of reality. She weaned herself down to one-eighth of that particular prescription. She chose to live with a higher level of pain by reducing her intake of that particular opioid. She soon started feeling like herself again, regaining her mental and emotional faculties. I stood back in stunned amazement at that time because, as a former drug user myself, I knew how very few people are ever able to do what Amy had just done. The woman is *a boss*. She went to war against her circumstances and she won. **It was during this time frame that Amy became my hero.** To this very day, she still is. There is nobody whom I admire on earth more than my wife.

The next few months were a complete overhaul of our lives. Nothing was the same, nor would it ever be. The Lord harnessed what Satan meant for our demise, and in authentic God-like fashion, He turned it for our good. We were walking together as a family through the most physically broken and most spiritually beautiful season. Physical therapy was torture for Amy. She went to every scheduled appointment, stubbornly determined to learn to walk again. I will never forget how I cried tears of joy when I watched her take those first steps on a walker at the rehabilitation facility. Soon, she walked with a cane. She would tell me that she was doing most of what she was doing for her children. She would not give in to her deep grief over her mom, her constant physical pain, her diagnosis of PTSD from the violent experience of the wreck, or the long, arduous process of learning how to be mobilized again. **The warrior won every battle.**

I am telling you the truth when I testify that I cannot remember her complaining once.
She never expressed one bitter word toward God.
She prayed and cried out to God night and day from her hospital bed in our den.
She read her Bible.
She read her mother's journals that Amy's dad brought to the house.
She kept doing all she knew to do: loving and trusting her Heavenly Father.
And she never stopped singing.

Through this terrible experience, Amy found out that mystery which many Christians assume is true about themselves, namely, that their faith in God is authentic and runs deep down to who they truly are. Amy learned that she really did love God more than anyone and anything else. She learned that she could testify of His glorious goodness through shadows of excruciating physical and emotional suffering with tears of her impossible grief. Amy crossed the threshold of deep, soul-bruising loss and still retained her delight in Jesus.

Amy is a real Christian. She's my favorite.

CHAPTER 22

Holy Spirit Takeover

"Our God is in the heavens; He does all that He pleases."
- Psalm 115:3

AMY AND I, SHORTLY AFTER she started to incrementally resume life as a wife and mom, began to experience a measurable acceleration in our spiritual lives. Something had shifted in the midst of our long and painful season of upheaval. Both of us began to gain a crystalized awareness of what was important and what was no longer that important. The religious pettiness that had been hammering away at us through battles with other Christians soon became an opposing force that we refused to tolerate any longer. Please understand the great majority of people in our church at this time were wonderful. They rallied around our family in our hour of need. It is still to this day the most lavish display of Christian compassion and action that I have ever personally witnessed as they helped us in countless ways for the first eighteen months after the car wreck. We were and are still incredibly grateful to all who came alongside our family. Having said that, there were a handful of goats among those sheep, and these few people, goats being what they are, engaged into stubborn headbutting with me about a variety of issues in the church. I just refused to validate their pettiness, and I stopped signing up for *death by papercut* as a pastor. I just decided no longer to lend credence to people in the church who wanted to pick me to death about their complaints, preferences, demands, or protests. I simply began to let them walk away from both me and the church. I no longer invested long hours trying to reason with them. Lots of them left once they realized that I was no longer going to invest time entertaining their moans. **Truthfully, some people in churches are simply unreasonable. They will never change.**

If you are a pastor or leader in a church, you need to know that.

You can put out their current flames of discontent through negotiation, give-and-take, and patient cooperation, but then they soon just find something new in which to be disgruntled. Some people live for drama, and others live to be in control. Pastors and church leaders are wise to invite these types of people to leave and search out a different place to "exercise their gifting." As this new season found me, I found myself willing to just allow people to be wrong, and I no longer felt compelled to debate with them or to validate their discontent. This was a difficult season for me as God continued to break me of my longing to be properly understood by others. He was crushing my orphan-spirited need to never have people leave me or my ministry. There were stacked months when I would walk into my house after a discouraging day at the church and have next to nothing in my tank to offer to my wife and children. Amy, Alicia, and Landon paid the price, for sure. What I did not realize at the time was that God was crucifying me. *I was dying to Jeff. I was dying to the opinions of others.* The Father was hammering sanctifying nails of execution into the parts of me that still longed to be respected, understood, and beloved by other people. Crucifixion was utilized by the ancient Romans as a means of slow, painful death. The victims usually did not bleed out. They suffocated there on their crosses – that is how most of them actually succumbed in the end. Crucifixion was designed to prolong the agony of the one on the cross. When Scripture says that we have been crucified with Christ, we do well to remember that it is a long, slow, and very painful spiritual process. **Dying to self is agony.** It does not happen in an instant. Spiritual crucifixion is a process that repeatedly brings us to the end of ourselves. We can never become like our Savior without the sanctification of our assigned crosses. Yes, it hurts, and I was learning that on a new and very intense level.

But I was growing closer to Jesus and finding renewed strength in the Holy Spirit. I was figuring it out as I went.

Though she was slowed by her injuries, Amy was a new woman in many ways. We moved away from our home in Lawrenceville that was very near to the scene of the wreck. God provided a nice home for us to spend the next few years. Alicia and Landon had to grow up fast due to the intensity that found our lives through the aftermath of losing Amy's mother and Amy losing much of her initial ability to take care of the children like she was used to doing. Do not get me wrong, she was 100% available to them emotionally and maternally, but her body could no longer do things like running, climbing, or playing outdoors with them. Alicia instinctively took up some of the things her mommy could no longer do. Alicia is so maternally gifted herself that Landon benefitted from his big sister's care for him. Landon's outlet for the struggles that had found him at such a young age became humor. By the time he was done with first grade, he had a clear gift for comedic timing, and much like me and my own dad, Landon displayed a natural gifting to make people laugh. What a gift he was (and is!) to our family. He kept us in stitches in what was otherwise a deeply challenging and prolonged season of continuing battle. God was overtly gracious to all four of us Lyles. Amid human opposition, circumstantial heaviness, sanctifying weakness, and regular battles with the enemy, God was infusing us with growing levels of grace and power in the Holy Spirit. We were all living out as a family the Apostle Paul's famous words from 2nd Corinthians 4:16-17, **"So we do not lose heart. Though our outer self is wasting away, our inner self is being renewed day by day. For this light momentary affliction is preparing for us an eternal weight of glory beyond all comparison."**

Behind the scenes, amid all the challenges I continued to face with people in the church, the Spirit of God was gaining more and more territory in my formerly reluctant heart. A trip to Africa further cemented in my heart the call of God to embrace the ways and gifts of the Holy Spirit. By this time, I had become fully surrendered to God concerning the gifts of the Spirit, and I had eagerly welcomed the return of the gift of tongues to my life. Nobody knew it, but I had been praying in tongues nearly every day as I now believed that I actually needed this practice in order to align with the truth of Jude 1:20, which connects praying in the Spirit with the ability to be strengthened in the faith. I traveled to Tanzania with a group of conservative pastors, leaders, and teachers who all came from a theological camp that stood staunchly against anything that remotely smacked of Charismatic Christianity. They were good men, for sure. Yet, I was definitely in the midst of differing viewpoints concerning the gifts of the Holy Spirit. As my norm had become, I simply kept my views and practices to myself and chose not to debate with my brothers.

Ironically, when we arrived in the city where we were training the African pastors, it turned out that the group who had networked to bring us there was the **Association of Pentecostal Ministers** in the city of Moshi, Tanzania! God had placed me, a tongue-talking Baptist pastor in a group of cessationist theologians to travel to Africa to train Pentecostal Africans in the art of expositional Bible preaching! You cannot make this stuff up. At the end of the week, I was given the task of presenting a study Bible to every attendee of the training conference. As the long line formed, I began to feel deeply stirred in my spirit. I knew that God wanted me to speak life and blessing over everyone who received a Bible. Suddenly, with each person who took a Bible from my hand, words began to drop supernaturally down from my mind and up from my heart through my lips and into their ears. I shared words of knowledge over people whom I had never met. There were close to two hundred leaders who moved through that line in the African heat that day — and each one of them received a prophetic word from an undercover Charismatic Baptist pastor from America. Many were stunned at the level of accuracy with which I was empowered to speak into their lives through the translator. Never before had I experienced such a deeply fulfilling two hours in ministry. Knowing that I was being used by God to build up others in the Body of Christ was such a treasure to me. God unlocked prophetic gifting in me on that afternoon, and when I returned to America, the gift was still flowing. **To this very day, I still find more satisfaction operating in the gift of prophecy than I do the gift of teaching.** Both are beautiful, but there is something about the prophetic word being released that impacts both the one speaking and the one receiving in indescribable ways. God was ushering me into a season where He was imparting new gifts to me.

Frankly, I had more flow happening inside me than I had the opportunity to release outside of me. It was the beginning of something beautiful.

Amy was also beginning to move in the gifts of the Spirit at this time. We had a long conversation one night over dinner at our favorite restaurant wherein I unpacked everything that happened to me over the last several years as it pertained to the supernatural gifts of the Spirit. Amy was deeply disappointed that I had not previously been open about these experiences with tongues, but she forgave me of my fear that she would not have been able to receive it from me without judging me. Soon, we began to note that she was flowing in a strangely precise prophetic gifting wherein she would get a word from the Lord, speak it out loud, and then whatever she spoke would come to pass in a short time afterward. As Baptists, we had always used phrases like, "The Lord laid it on my heart to tell you…" or "Hey, friend, I could not get you off my mind today, and thought I should call you…" We had never used Charismatic vocabulary, but we had always believed in the gift of discernment. What we came to learn is that we had believed much more in the gifts of the Spirit than we ever realized. We just had always used different words to describe these gifts. **Ironically, we never used the actual Bible terms for these gifts**. Prophecy, word of wisdom, or word of knowledge just sounded too Charismatic for us, so, as good Baptists, we made up our own less controversial words to describe the same type of activity. That is so funny to me now! As Amy began to flow in her prophetic discernment and declarations, we came to the conclusion as a couple that God was doing something significant *in us* because He intended to do something significant *through us*.

What was happening to the Lyles?

People close to us were asking that very question. They could not quite put their finger on it, but they sensed something different in Amy's worship leading and my preaching. Our television audience started sending me emails and notes detailing that they were sensing something distinct in my pulpit ministry. Because much of our television audience was comprised of Charismatic Christians who found us after looking for more in-depth Bible teaching, we soon started seeing an increase in the number of visitors at Meadow Baptist who operated in the gifts of the Spirit. Frankly, they were confused by what they experienced when they visited the church. They sensed that I, as the pastor, had a different touch on my life than did the rest of the church's ministries. It wasn't a matter of good versus bad. It was just a difference that they noted and eventually communicated to me. God began to use these recurring conversations with these precious people to awaken me to His intention to take what He had done inside of me over the previous several years and offer it to the entire church family. God was pushing me out of the safety of my ministerial nest. He was moving me to fly by faith and to begin to instruct our congregation about the gifts of the Holy Spirit. Honestly, I was not looking forward to this. After years of being rejected by church members for merely doing away with their non-biblical traditions, what would happen when I actually started dismantling our church's historical doctrinal stance against the gifts of the Holy Spirit? We were taught that those gifts had ceased. *That belief was actually encoded in our church doctrinal statement and bylaws!* If people had been upset enough to leave over silly denominational traditions, what would happen if I began to topple the sacred theological altars of disbelief in the Holy Spirit gifts?

Yet, it was clear to me that God was not *asking me* to do this. He was *telling me* that I was going to do it. Years before, I had refused Him when He had offered me a new and clear pathway in the Spirit. I had suffered for that fearful disobedience. I would not be doing that again. **God is in Heaven and does whatever He pleases. He does not ask permission.** Sometimes, He refuses to wait on our reluctance. I began to see that this was a right-now word from the Lord.

I began to pray about how to obey what I knew would be a delicate and risky endeavor. Once again, the sovereign God of Heaven was taking me into waters far above my head.

CHAPTER 23

A Baptism of Courage

"And now, Lord, look upon their threats and grant to Your servants to continue to speak Your word with all boldness..."
- Acts 4:29

I WISH YOU COULD MEET Jude. When he introduced himself to me in the sanctuary at Meadow Baptist, I immediately knew I had made a friend. Jude is a large man from Nigeria with a silent, strong presence like no other man I have ever met. Power oozes from his spiritual pores. His thick Nigerian accent makes everything that comes out of his mouth sound even a little more dynamic. We struck up a relationship that was so pivotal for me at that particular time. He was among those who kept coming to Meadow while privately wondering what in the world they were doing there. Jude was a pastor in Nigeria with strong gifting in the prophetic. Because overt spiritism is prevalent in his hometown in Africa, Jude was amazingly comfortable describing his encounters with demons, witchdoctors, occultists, and the spiritual forces of darkness. I had never had ongoing access to a *real-live Charismatic* like Jude. We spent long hours together as he let me ask him endless questions on matters in which I was confused and skeptical. In turn, he received from me a challenge to harmonize what he believed and experienced with God's Word. Jude was the first person I ever prayed with out loud in tongues. We would prophesy to each other in his little office at the church which I financially helped him plant. It was such an enriching relationship and one which I desperately needed. Jude definitely stretched me well outside of my theological comfort zone, but we were mutually blessed in each other's company. That is why he was the first person I called when God allowed another intense crisis of ministry to land squarely in my lap.

Arriving home from a conference in Minnesota, my phone began to blow up as soon as I turned it back on after my plane landed. There were three religious powerbrokers in the church who all, independently of one another, had been aggressively resisting my leadership while I was away at the conference. Yes, I was gone for five days, and in my absence, three men decided to try and facilitate a coup of my leadership. I was instantly impacted and felt trapped between wanting to run in fear or fight these brothers in my flesh. I called Jude, and he agreed to meet me in my office to pray. An hour later, he was seated across from me, his big frame filling out an armchair where he listened patiently to my sob story. **I was tired of fighting these men. I was weary of my leadership being attacked.** I began to cry tears of exhaustion from years of having to battle for every square foot of advance that God offered to me at the church. When would I be free from the religious spirit that dominated our church? When would my opposition be removed by God? Honestly, I was crumbling right there in the presence of my brother from Nigeria. He watched me as I whined and wept for thirty solid minutes about these three men in the church who were gunning for me.

If you know anything about Nigerian prophets, you know that they don't play around. They are bold as lions and fierce with the fire of God. In the midst of my pitiful crying, I heard Jude shout out in his thick African accent, "Man of God!!! Stop your crying right now. Stop it! WE WILL PRAY!" What occurred in the next half hour is still one of the most supernatural events I have ever experienced. If you struggled with my account of receiving the gift of tongues in the earlier part of this book, you should buckle up for what I am about to tell you. I promise you that it is true. I have no idea if what I experienced was in the natural realm or the realm of the Spirit. Maybe it was both – I simply do not know. Here is what played out in my office after Jude authoritatively summoned me to wipe my tears, cease from whimpering, and engage in warfare prayer alongside him. The prophet from Nigeria took control of the room.

Jude began to call out to God for a baptism of courage for me. He prayed some highly Africanized prayers that used poetic language involving the removal of demonic spirits from Meadow. He spoke a curse against the spirits of rebellion and religion at work in the three men who were underhandedly fighting against me. Jude called on God to break them in that very moment and bring them to repentance. I remember him declaring that, should they not be willing to repent, that they would be "yanked up instantly by their roots" and removed from the church. **He then rebuked the spirit of fear at work in me. He called out the orphan spirit in me and powerfully spoke sonship into my life.** Somewhere in the midst of all that he was saying, Jude began to pray loudly in tongues. I began weeping as I joined him in praying in the Spirit. It was at this peak of spiritual saturation in the room when I opened my eyes. While we were praying together, I had felt like I was in a different place other than my office, so I opened my eyes just to physically orient to where I was.

This is where I could no longer tell if what I was seeing was natural or supernatural.

My whole office was clouded with a thin, white mist. It was cool on my skin, bright white, and basically transparent. I would describe it as a haze, but it had more texture than a haze. It was bright, but unlike light, it had dimension to it. It was not as defined as snow, but it was fuller than fog. I was astounded for about ten seconds, and then I became aware that Jude's prayers had transitioned back into English. He made a series of potent declarations over me and then called me to enter into declarations of faith about the opposition I was experiencing. My heart was racing as I repeated bold statements of victory over the three men's schemes to undermine my leadership. *I renounced fear. I renounced my former state of allowing myself to be intimidated by them. I committed to obeying the Lord's directions without hesitation.* Not long after this, Jude and I sealed our prayers by invoking the name of Jesus over everything we had asked, declared, and believed. When I opened my eyes and stood up, **I was filled with a new and measurable courage.** The white mist was dissipating but still visible to me. I know that sounds insane to some of you reading, but I can only tell you that I truly experienced it as the presence of God had been filling me and the room in which I sat. Jude remained in his chair and listened in as I reached out to each of the three men on my office phone and called them into accountability over what they had been doing while I was away at the conference. Not surprisingly, none of them delighted in what I was telling them. I exposed their underhanded schemes to each of them. I called them to meet with me and the elders to lay everything out in public that they had been slanderously advancing in private, whispered conversations. Operating in a fresh endowment from the Holy Spirit that had just been given me, I felt zero traces of fear. Righteousness was ruling my heart and mind again, and the fear of man had been entirely removed from me. The spiritual weariness was also completely gone. Something had shifted again within me, and I had been fully delivered from tolerating religiously spirited people in the church. I drew a line in the sand with each of the men and empowered them to respond to the parameters I had just established with them. The best vocabulary I can use for this experience that day is that I received a very specific baptism of the Holy Spirit that permanently transitioned me out of fearing the religious spirit in our church. I had been waging war against dead religion for years by this point, but I understood at that moment that I had been fighting it, at least partially, in sinful and self-protective fear. In my prayer time with Jude, the battle had now become about faith. Fear had been forced to pack its bags and vacate the premises. A white mist of courage had ushered it out the door.

Within two months, all three of those men quietly left the church. That day in my office broke a heavy and suffocating spiritual yoke off of me and also off of the ministry given to me. The yoke was fully removed, but it took a little while to pull out of me all the splinters it left on my shoulders. God sent a Nigerian prophet to a suburban Baptist church to set a struggling pastor free from the fear of the flock – *hallelujah!* It would not be the final battle I would experience with rebellion and religion at Meadow, but it was a breakthrough that left me permanently equipped with the understanding and courage to know how to deal with these types of controlling personalities in ministry.

God had baptized me with courage. He gave me back the boldness that I had unknowingly fumbled some time before that day. I had been craving a baptism of clarity from Him. Instead, He gave me a baptism of *courage*. By His grace, it still drips off of me today.

CHAPTER 24
Coming Out of the Charismatic Closet

"For I did not shrink from declaring to you the whole counsel of God."
– Acts 20:27

AFTER SPENDING NEARLY ALL MY Christian life doing things *for God*, I began to learn how to do everything *with God*. That is not to say that there was not some periodic bouncing back and forth between the *for God* and *with God* dynamic, but I now understood that there was a difference between the two.

> Constantly doing things *for God* brings results, but it leaves us hollow and weary.
> Doing things *with God* also brings results, but we are refreshed along the way as we operate in His power, patience, and freedom.
>
> Doing things *for God* impresses religious people.
> Doing things *with God* can actually upset religious people.
>
> Doing things *for God* allows us to claim some of the glory on earth.
> Doing things *with God* eradicates our desire for any glory. We prefer not to be noticed when we do things with Him.
>
> Doing things *for God* can leave us trusting in our own level of discipline, our own spiritual gifts, and our own experiences.
> Doing things *with God* allows us to open-handedly surrender all of our disciplines, gifts, and experiences and to humbly know that those things are worthless apart from Him.

For the first time in about twenty years of being a Jesus follower, I was now learning to do life and ministry with Him. *It was a wee bit of an awesome experience for me.*

The time had arrived for me to begin to lead the church out of our unquestioned denominational norms and into a radical embrace of the whole counsel of God. Lots of Christians and churches say that they are Bible-believing. I have found that many of those who say so are actually not. They believe the Bible up to the very point where the proper interpretation of the words of Scripture begins to cut cross-grain against their traditionally held beliefs. When it comes to the gifts of the Holy Spirit, it is obvious to me that we have some major inconsistencies among those who declare themselves to be *sola scriptura, biblically allegiant* saints. My personal commitment to let my Bible define my beliefs had served me well my entire Christian life. It empowered me to expose non-biblical traditions. Jesus once declared over a group of deeply religious leaders, **"These people worship me in vain; their teachings are merely human rules that they pass off as the very commandments of God."** It is nothing new to recognize that human religious traditions, once they have been passed on without examination from generation to generation, start sounding as if they are the very words of God. My denomination had taught me that the gifts of the Holy Spirit ceased around the end of the first century. Never mind that the Bible does not teach that doctrine, it was unilaterally taught as fact to me by every pastor, professor, and mentor I ever had. These were good men, but they were flat out wrong on this issue. God had led me to examine this type of teaching by measuring it against the words of Scripture.

Do you know what I discovered?

There is not one single verse in all of the Bible that teaches that the gifts ceased at the end of the first century. *Not a single verse.* There is, however, a copious number of verses that establish the value of all of the gifts of the Holy Spirit for the Body of Christ. The gifts of the Holy Spirit were no small side dish to the early Christians. They were front and center in how the Christians worshipped, served, prayed, and advanced the Gospel. The Holy Spirit gifts were an absolute necessity to our spiritual ancestors in the Church. We now have massive numbers of believers and entire denominations who have unilaterally concluded that those gifts are no longer necessary, therefore, they are no longer available.

> *The early Christians needed the gifts of the Spirit.*
> *The early Christians possessed the gifts of the Spirit.*
> *The early Christians received and operated in the gifts of the Spirit.*
> *The early Christians sometimes misused and abused the gifts of the Spirit.*
> *The early Christians were commanded to ongoingly desire and pursue the gifts of the Spirit.*

The early Christians prophesied, spoke in tongues, interpreted tongues, moved in miracles, communicated words of supernatural knowledge and wisdom, healed people, cast out demons, served sacrificially, gave generously, taught via the spirit of wisdom and revelation, and endured deep trials through supernaturally empowered steadfastness. They also relied immensely on apostolic doctrine – the teachings which would eventually become our New Testament. **The early Church was not forced to choose between reliance upon revealed truth or embracing of supernatural gifts of the Holy Spirit.** They needed both and embraced both as being essential for fruitful lives and ministry. Did not Jesus teach that the Father was seeking those who would worship Him in Spirit and Truth? Can we possibly believe that we are allowed to choose one and decline the other? *God forbid.*

Less than a year after the Father moved out those three men who had caused me so much angst, the sense of God's call to teach our church about Holy Spirit gifts became insuppressible within me. After much prayer and fasting, I called an elders' meeting, and I asked my fellow leaders at Meadow Baptist Church to lend me their ears for a couple of hours one night. In that meeting, I told them that I believed our church bylaws were flagrantly out of alignment with the Bible on the subject of spiritual gifts. Decades earlier, Meadow had encoded in our statement of faith that we stood against the contemporary manifestation of the supernatural gifts. **Those words had been in our bylaws for over forty years.** I let those brothers know that the Holy Spirit was leading me to teach in an expositional manner on the subject of spiritual gifts, just like I had been doing on all other theological matters for the twelve previous years as the pastor of Meadow. They agreed that it would make sense that I should teach through 1st Corinthians, chapters twelve through fourteen, to bring Scriptural light on the matter. Everyone was on the same page in that meeting when we left. Two Sundays later, I shared the first of what would eventually be thirteen separate messages at Meadow Baptist Church on the gifts of the Holy Spirit. **By the time I got to the fourth message, two of the elders nervously called the rest of us into a meeting with them.** They had listened to my messages and were genuinely struggling with my affirmation of the supernatural gifts as being available and necessary for modern Christians today. These two men were more than twenty-five years older than me and had both been Lead Pastors in conservative Baptist churches in previous decades. They wanted me to reel in my series on the spiritual gifts. Frankly, they wanted me to stop preaching on the subject entirely. Repeatedly in the meeting, I was gently warned by these two brothers that what I was teaching about Holy Spirit gifts was in violation of the church bylaws.

My response was to tell them that the church bylaws were in violation of the eternal Word of God.

I begged both of them to biblically refute anything they had heard me teach on the matter. They both acknowledged that they could not refute my position by using the Bible. One of them told me that he could not use the Bible to prove that the gifts of the Spirit had ceased but that it did not matter because *he knew that he was right.* I literally began to shed tears when this dear man, a man whom I respected and loved, made that statement. **I realized then that this conflict was spiritual war between man's religion and God's revelation.** When they continued to hold the bylaws over my head, trying to force me to stop preaching the truth about the gifts, I realized that there was no way out. Rather than splitting our church in two over the issue of the gifts of the Holy Spirit, I adjourned the meeting and asked that we pray for a few days and then reconvene. Everyone agreed. We needed to seek the Lord.

I spent a couple of days seeking God's heart on what I was to do. I knew that He was the One who prompted me to come out of the closet about my views on the gifts of the Spirit. He called me to go public with my views. He summoned me out of fear, reluctance, and embarrassment over being a Baptist who both treasured the Word AND the gifts. I tapped freshly into that ongoing baptism of courage, and I discerned that I could not retreat and stop preaching the sermon series on the gifts. By the way, many people in the church were growing excited and encouraged about what they were hearing in that sermon series. Some of those who were — already part of the Meadow family had been waiting for this series for years — as they were also privately walking in the gifts of the Spirit. There was a — holy stir in the church as the series had been continuing each Sunday. If I quit the series now and bowed to our church by-laws, I believe I would have permanently entrenched a reputation as another man-pleasing pastor, and God would have removed my candlestick from the church. When the elders got back together, I told them I would continue the series as planned on the upcoming Sunday. There was pushback and pleading from these men. Please know that these were not bad men. They loved Jesus. They served Him well. I think they loved me too. It just came to pass that we could not agree on the right steps to take. While I did not agree to stop preaching the series, I did offer to resign as Lead Pastor in order to avoid dividing the church. One of the brothers told me that my doing so would rupture the church and consequently leave the elders with too big of a mess to clean up in my absence. They did not wish to do that.

So, the two elders who disagreed the strongest with me on the matter passed across the table their already prepared and signed resignations from continuing as elders of Meadow.

They could no longer follow me. They believed me to be in theological error, even though I could substantiate my position with clear Bible

teaching. They, while acknowledging that they could not support their own
— position with clear Scripture, chose their tradition over God's truth on the
matter of the gifts of the Holy Spirit. They chose religion over revelation.
They chose the bylaws over the Bible.

And then they left the church.

When all was said and done a few months later, one-third of our congregation
left with these two men. Some nasty stuff happened after their calm
resignations in the meeting that night. Frankly, it got ugly on one of their
ends. The Lord intensely instructed me not to fight back and to pour out
my complaint only to Him and my wife. When some underhanded activity
continued even after they left, I prayed and received permission from the
Lord to call one of the two men. I had been closest to this brother in the
past. I asked him to please stop sowing discord, and I basically begged him
to cease and desist from some of what he and his wife had been doing after
their departure. He agreed to stop, and we prayed over the phone for God
to help us love one another as we went our separate ways in ministry. Within
a week, the same activity resumed by both him and his wife, and I realized
that there was nothing more for me to do. My heart was broken, but I must
say, *my spirit was so stirred* about what we could do now that the church was
liberated from the spirit of religion that had been so prevalent for so long.
I had not become bitter. I did not fight flesh with flesh. I chose not to hide
the full counsel of God from the flock and I finished preaching the sermon
series. **The church came alive almost immediately after the large
exodus following behind these two former leaders.** We had weathered
the spiritual storm and had come through as one body committed to the
truth of the Word and eagerly desiring the gifts of the Holy Spirit. It was
an amazing relaunch of who we were as a community of believers. We did
not have as many people as we once did. We lost a lot of faithful givers
when the exodus was complete, so the church finances were not strong.
Some who remained with us at Meadow were bruised and a little relationally
fragile after witnessing two of the five elders walk away, but they stayed and
waited to see what the Father would do. It was hard for all of us, for sure.

But hard does not necessarily mean bad. We were all figuring that out as we went.

We were free as a church family and God began to smile on us immediately. He almost always does when we trust Him, obey in tough assignments, and refuse to fight in the flesh when we are opposed. Some of you reading are walking out a season in which God is calling you to courage. He is showing you a better way, but you know that there is a cost associated with it. The comfort zone is screaming at you not to forsake it. It makes you promises if you will just remain there, but the Holy Spirit is calling you out of comfort and deeper into courage and consecration. Your heart is being stirred, and He is not allowing you to settle it back down. God wants to rain down something new upon you. **He is inviting you to close a door behind you and walk through the one He is opening in front of you.** God looks for people who will do these types of things, *courageous things*. He has something special awaiting people like that – people like you. I was soon to find out what this looked like in my own life and ministry.

God was going to take me across a threshold that would usher me into the season for which I was made. Everything up to this point was leading up to the moment that unfolds in the next chapter.

CHAPTER 25

Waiting on a Word to Ripen

*"The LORD is good to those who wait for Him, to the soul who seeks Him.
It is good that one should wait quietly for the salvation of the LORD."*
– Lamentations 3:25-26

ABOUT TWO YEARS AFTER I was saved, I was living in a large house in a suburb of Atlanta called Dacula. A friend had moved out of this house to a different city and was struggling to sell it. Rather than traveling back regularly to take care of the yard and ensure the house was occupied, he rented it to me for an extremely low price. It was an amazing season for me as I had comfortable surroundings and lots of solitude in the big house as a single man running hard after Jesus. One afternoon, as I was praying upstairs in my bedroom, I fell to my knees under the sense of God's presence. I was a novice in all of the supernatural ways of the Lord at that time, and I was overwhelmed by the weightiness of His manifest presence in the room. As I wept in prayer, I heard in my human spirit the undeniable communication of the Holy Spirit, saying to me, **"Soon. It is coming. Soon."**

That was it. That was all I had heard, but I knew it was a level of clarity in the voice of the Lord that I had not experienced since my call to preach about eighteen months prior to that moment. For years after that supernatural word given to me in Dacula, I periodically wondered what He was referencing by that strong but unclarified whisper. Many times, I asked God, *"Is this it? Is this the it's-coming-soon fulfillment?"* He never said yes when I asked. Years went by without any confirmation that the word had ever been fulfilled. Through marriage, two children being born, coming on staff as a vocational pastor, being promoted to Lead Pastor, receiving the gift of tongues and other supernatural gifting…none of these things were the fulfillment of that word spoken to me on the floor of my bedroom in 1996. He just said that *something was coming* to me. I never forgot about what He said, but eventually, I just stopped asking Him if anything I was presently experiencing was the actual fulfillment. It was not that I ever doubted the word – I didn't. I just eventually concluded that, because I had received this personal word from God, then He would let me know when it was precisely fulfilled.

That moment arrived for me on the first Sunday of 2016.

Having turned the corner to theologically affirm the gifts of the Spirit at Meadow Baptist Church, we were now a faith-family that publicly committed to operating under the authority of the written Word and the necessity of the Holy Spirit. We no longer had to pick between honoring the Bible and operating in the power of the Spirit. Like the Christians of the first century, we happily embraced apostolic doctrine (Word) and the *charismata* (gifts of the Holy Spirit). It was a refreshing time. During the early days of this season, I met two men who would become such dear friends and brothers to me. Dustin Pennington pastored an Assemblies of God church in Dacula, interestingly, the very same city where I had received the personal word from God about something coming soon to me. Billy Humphrey had established, right down the street from where I served at Meadow, the second of only two 24/7 houses of prayer in the entire United States. My relationship with these two men was initially just one of encouraging brotherhood. Dustin is a relational dynamo, and Billy carries a heavy mantle of leadership in the Kingdom. As one who had been repeatedly burned by numerous men in the Church, I was delighted to have two new friends with no strings attached. **We were just brothers with nothing to prove and nothing to lose. It was freedom.** I learned quickly that both of these guys also cherished the Word and the Spirit as I did. Billy answered so many questions from me about my concerns of excesses and abuses among Charismatic Christians. Though I affirmed and moved in the supernatural gifts, I intentionally maintained a distance from what would be called the Charismatic Movement. I was not then (and am not now) looking to join a human movement. I just long for truth and fullness in the

153

Kingdom. Billy helped me work through much of my skepticism about the concerns I had about the world of *charismania*. Dustin helped me navigate healing from the relational bruises which I had encountered as a pastor. In this relationship with these two men, I felt that I had gained a Barnabas in Dustin and a Paul in Billy. Together, my two friends reopened me to the biblical call to authentic brotherhood among Christian men. Sometimes, the Father sends the right people at the right time. For the first time in a very long time, I was making friends.

When Dustin invited me to lead a weekend men's offsite retreat for his church, I agreed to pray about it. I was not taking many outside engagements during that time; however, something felt right about this request from Dustin. When Amy told me that she also really felt I needed to do it, I called Dustin and happily agreed to share with his men at the retreat. Dustin is a bridge builder, and it meant a lot to me for him to risk inviting the Baptist guy to lead a retreat with a bunch of Pentecostal men at an offsite location. The weekend was really healthy and encouraging. God moved in the worship and the Word, and I thoroughly enjoyed my first official time of ministering in a Charismatic atmosphere. I preached four times on the life of Moses in thirty-six hours, and then I headed back home to get ready for Sunday services at Meadow while Dustin led his men in the final session on Saturday night. My friendship with Dustin was growing, and I felt honored to be allowed to pour into his flock.

Sunday evening, I received a text from Dustin asking me to meet in the morning at my office. He said that he needed to run something by me. When he showed up the next morning, I could tell that something was churning and burning within him. He prefaced what he was about to share with a request for me to hear him out and unless something inside me leapt at what he said, he did not want me to entertain what he was about to share. Highly intrigued, I agreed and then listened as Dustin recounted an inner vision that he had experienced after his Sunday morning service the day before. In the vision, the Holy Spirit had supernaturally communicated to him that he was to lay down his pastoral ministry at Cornerstone Fellowship.

Additionally, he said that the same vision included a communication that — I was going to lay down my own ministry at Meadow. *Dustin had my full* — *attention at this point.* Then, the Lord brought Dustin to understand that both laid down ministries would be raised back up as one new ministry. God wanted to marry Meadow Baptist Church and Cornerstone Assemblies of — God Fellowship and make us into a visible signal of Kingdom unity to our — region. *Sounds utterly ridiculous, right? The Baptists and Pentecostals merging into one? Can oil and water embrace?*

Apparently, when it is the water of the Word and the oil of the Spirit, the answer is yes.

What Dustin could never have known is that a few days before I preached to the men of his church, I was sitting in a restaurant with a church planter in our county. As Rolando and I enjoyed some good Cuban food together, I had confessed to him that I felt like God wanted me to search out a church that adhered to a commitment to both the written Word of God — and the gifts of the Holy Spirit. I remember saying to Rolando, "Surely — there is a church in our city that promotes the authority of the Bible and necessity of spiritual gifts." Like 99% of other ministers would have replied, Rolando chuckled and said, "Good luck with that merger quest, Jeff." I knew it sounded silly, but I really felt like it was a God-birthed desire that was inside of me. That was on the Tuesday before the men's retreat. Here I was now, six days later, and Dustin was in my office sharing a vision God gave him about he and I laying our individual ministries before the Lord and trusting God to raise them up as one new merged work for His name's sake. The Holy Spirit indeed began leaping within my human spirit as I felt an unction on what Dustin was sharing. We committed to fast and pray and then discuss it more on Friday.

By Friday, we knew the merger was from the Lord and we both said yes. Much work would need to take place and many more voices would need to be invited to speak into the process. In the end, not a single leader in Cornerstone or Meadow felt anything more than a holy permission from the Father to move forward in an unprecedented joining of two local churches across previously drawn denominational lines. **God was tearing down walls of religion in Atlanta and raising up a new bridge of unity.**

I won't bore you with the details, but suffice it to say, a little less than four full months later, Cornerstone Fellowship had de-constituted, sold their building and property, and had brought over 99% of their existing members to join Meadow Baptist Church. During that first merged Sunday service between the two congregations, the Holy Spirit spoke to me and said,

"I told you it was coming soon. This is it. This is what I have been preparing you for, Jeff." It was the first Sunday of 2016, and that long-ago spoken word from 1996 was now being fulfilled before my very eyes. The fruit had ripened, and I was getting my first taste of what God had brought forth.

For the next year, Dustin and I both endured and enjoyed the ups and downs of merging two very different faith families. It was not as hard as one might have assumed. There was so much grace on what we were doing that the atmosphere was consistently one of joy and momentum in the Spirit. Not everyone made it through this radical commitment to unity. Good people had to move on from us during this time. Nobody caused any lasting fuss when doing so, and as their pastors, Dustin and I completely understood that this was deeply challenging for them. Merging churches is not for the faint of heart – whether you are a pastor or a church member. My hope is that God will eventually allow me to write an entire book on what took place during the two merges of which I was a part.

Yes, that is correct: I said **two** merges.

Not quite a year and a half into the merge of Cornerstone and Meadow, our newly named church, now called New Bridge Church, entered into another fresh offer from Heaven. Through yet another dream which God imparted to Dustin, he, Billy and I answered the call to merge New Bridge

156

and the Atlanta International House of Prayer into a mission base that would unite local church ministry with the global prayer movement. The cement on our first merger had not even settled before we three brothers were back on our faces seeking wisdom from God about how to do what He was calling us to do.

Please know that, although the source of origin for the two merges were two separate supernatural encounters that Dustin experienced with God, we took great strides in fasting and prayer to ensure we were properly responding to those dreams. This second merger took eight months to fully complete. We sought input from our broader leadership teams. We spoke with trusted friends and mentors in other parts of the country. We spent many long, tiring hours assessing the legal components of what we were doing. We dialogued in sometimes painful humility about how our roles would work as three men who were used to leading from the first chair. I, perhaps more than Dustin and Billy, struggled during the second merger. Billy carries a strong apostolic leadership mantle. His role and my role overlapped in multiple areas where there would be room for only one man to run point. Fortunately, we were no longer young leaders tempted to fight for self. God made it plain to all three of us how our roles would be defined and that, if we would pursue love and humility, there would not be any points of conflict that we could not overcome together. **Our amazing Father has been true to His word to us unto this very day.** At the time of this writing, our twice-merged mission base is thriving with a healthy local church ministry anchored in night and day, nonstop prayer, with a global missions outreach that has dispatched more than fifty missionaries to the nations straight from our own faith family. The prayer movement had said yes to the local church, and the local church had re-centered itself in prayer just like the early Christians did as evidenced in our New Testament. This is what community and ministry was supposed to be.

God's promise to me has fully ripened. I am enjoying the taste of every bite of this savory Kingdom fruit. I knew just a few months after my radical conversion that God had called me into ministry. That was all that I knew.

I was summoned to preach by the sovereign God of Heaven, and that calling both awed and terrified me, but I did it. I did what I knew to do. That calling to preach became more clarified a few years later when it flowed into a call to pastor a flock. That also awed and terrified me, but I did it. I again did what I knew to do, even though I did not know exactly how to do it. **I knew I would figure it out as I went along, trusting and obeying the will of God.** I knew that He would teach me and help me. From 2002 to 2016, I did my best to follow the One who was leading me. There were so many mistakes that I made along the way. To this day, I have some deep regrets about some of the ways I did things. Most of it, however, was done well as I gave Him my best. Sometimes there was precision, sometimes there was passion. In many good seasons, *there were both*.

If God had told me that it would take more than twenty years from my original calling to my awareness that I had finally stepped into the fullness of that calling, I am unsure that I would have said yes to Him. He is so wise not to disclose to us more than we can handle. Because of that, I have learned not to demand of Him *the when* and *the why* of things. The heights that He ordained were breathtaking for me. The depths which He also ordained were backbreaking. Through it all, my shepherding King was so very good to me. He is also good to you. **Maybe you yourself are wondering if it all will ever make sense.** Maybe you are reading this and frustrated at the length of time you have been made to wait. Maybe your desire for clarity in your life has become more important than His call to courage for your life. May I suggest something to you?

He wants you to walk with Him some more. He is calling you to continue with Him a little farther. He wants you to look to Him. **He wants you to know that there are simply some things you also must figure out as you go.**

Take it from a guy who is still on that journey. Yes, to this very moment, I am also still figuring it out as I go. It's so worth it.

CHAPTER 26

One Last Chapter: Some Things I Figured Out as I Went

"Get wisdom; get insight; do not forget, and do not turn away from the words of my mouth. Do not forsake her, and she will keep you; love her, and she will guard you."
- Proverbs 4:5-6

THERE IS AN OLD QUOTE from Oswald Chambers that still sticks with me. He once said, **"Faith never knows where it is being led, but it loves and knows the One who is leading."**

That's a good word, Brother Ozzie.

We are often addicted to our needing to know and understand what God is doing in our lives. Most of us believe that the more we know, the better prepared we are to succeed. That is because we usually have flawed definitions of *success*. We equate success with safety, material abundance, health, accomplishments, comfort, ease, leisure, and pleasure. I do not necessarily have an aversion to those things, but I have learned enough to know that they do not guarantee my success as a child of God. If I am honest, my experience has been that the more of those things I am experiencing, the more difficult it is for me to prosper in the Spirit. If I know everything that is coming my way and have all material provision to handle it once it arrives, then I really do not need faith, do I? *Where is there room for trusting God if I know everything I am going to face and if I have the ability to insulate myself from whatever it might require of me?* I believe it was also Oswald Chambers who quipped, **"We control all that we understand. Is it any wonder that we wish to understand everything?"**

My life has evolved as I have lived it. So has yours. In truth, our lives are still evolving. I began as a child who moved into being a *rebel*. Then, God in His

159

unimaginable mercy made me to become one who was *redeemed* through Jesus' sacrifice. After my redemption, I ignorantly became *religious,* and after the religious season ended, I found myself *released* into spiritual freedom through the Word and the Spirit. Based on experience, my guess is that I am ignorant today of some more things that I will figure out as I continue to go on in this amazing journey with the Father, learning His heart a little more with every step. **Life does not come with a complete syllabus, so please stop expecting it all to make sense.** I did not foresee my parents' divorce and my mother walking away from our family. It crushed my young heart, and I had to figure out how to respond to the pain as I continued on in my life. Addictions later owned me for so many years as I lived as a rebel – I never saw coming my way those dark years that I cultivated for myself. It took me a full decade to truly understand that this was the pitiful life which I had chosen and that it would never get better on its own. Time would <u>not</u> heal all those self-inflicted wounds. I needed the Healer to come to me, and He was waiting until my brokenness reached its ultimate depths in my soul. It was only then that I chose to surrender to His restoring, redeeming grace. That moment was a long time coming, and there was so much that I had to figure out along the way.

As a single man, newly saved, who so wanted to share his life with a woman of God, I had to figure out what to look for in a woman. I had it all wrong at first, but the grace of God soon aligned my heart with His, and I eventually met Amy. I still marvel that He let me marry her, but how would I ever experience breakthrough as a love-stuttering husband who struggled relationally with his wife? That answer was definitely something that I had to figure out along the way. The same process had to take place in my calling as a father to Alicia and Landon. Again, there was no syllabus, only the Word and the Spirit. There was no *six-steps-to-relational-dynamo* workbook. I had a wonderful Counselor and a heart commitment not to perpetually fail my family. I am still figuring out some of what all that means. I am figuring it out as I am walking it out.

When it comes to leading and serving God's people in Kingdom ministry, there are innumerable things that I now understand that, in those former years, I was utterly ignorant. **Understanding comes to us in stages.** You cannot leave a season with understanding until you have first entered that season without it. Wisdom and understanding ride into our lives on the backs of personal experiences with God. He works incrementally to bring about wisdom and maturity in His kids as we walk out the evolving seasons of life. I honestly did not always know how to do what God called me to do as a husband, father, pastor, servant, and leader. Rather than caving into the paralysis of analysis, I prayed, waited, and committed to God to do the very best that I knew how to do in each season, every struggle, and all my staggering. Most of the time, it worked out beautifully. Some of the time, it was a train wreck and people were wounded. There was a whole lot of pain and there were a few crisis points where I wanted to quit. Yet, God called me to press on for another day and keep figuring it out as I went. **Some amazing things come to all of us who refuse to stop pressing on.** Endurance is not glamorous. Perseverance does not come with polish. We need grace for sure…but we also need some *grit* if we ever hope to receive wisdom and understanding from God.

Sometimes the Christian life feels a little like *ready-fire-aim!* Faith does not provide us with everything upfront. We cannot always see the targets clearly. Jesus calls us out on the waves and trains us to lock eyes with Him while everything is crashing around us, against us, and at times, within us. Our fight or flight instinct often tries to kick in, and we either want to run back to the presumed safety of the boat or give in to despair that sinks us down into the churning waters of trouble that have wearied us. What we often forget is that those beckoning boats can still sink with us inside of them, and the churning waters will ultimately drown us if we surrender to them and quit. Whether we choose to run to some presumed place of safety or give up in abject despair, ultimately, we are acting in ways **that keep us in control.** It is easier to give up or scramble for safety than it is to continue to hold our fixed faith-gaze upon Jesus and wait for further instructions. While you stand still, knowing that He is God, **you are learning as you go.** It is okay not to have all the answers. Nobody is helped by all of the Church's silly, recycled clichés that are mindlessly passed on as if they were real answers. There are no Spirit-filled control freaks — those two descriptions are polar opposites. You and I were never supposed to have all the answers ahead of time. We are supposed to learn to live with large gaps in our present understanding. Those gaps are the places where God pours in our opportunities to trust Him, abide in His grace, and wait for glorious understanding to come. He ordains those blank spaces in our souls where things just do not make sense. **He brings us repeatedly to the end of our self-reliance.** He trains us to rejoice when we have zero control over things.

And it is not just me.

God is calling **you** to also give yourself to a life of figuring things out as you go. He is waiting for you to surrender to this reality that all of His children must embrace.

This is what faith looks like. Truly, this is what Christianity is supposed to look like for all of us.

Walking with Jesus is not Him saving you and then Him handing you a book that presumably tells you precisely what to expect and when to expect it for the rest of your days. That blessed book, the Bible, tells you *about Him.* It tells you who He is and what He is like. It is filled with a supernaturally churning mix of His promises, passions, precepts, priorities, principles, and prohibitions. The Bible is His self-revelation. It is His great gift to us.

But the Bible is not a book of detailed explanations about what you need to know in every situation. There is not a clear verse within its pages about everything that you are going to encounter in life. **The Bible is a magnet that draws us in closer to its Author so that we might know Him.** If He gave us all the answers ahead of time, human nature being what it is, we would just spend all our time studying print on page and very little time being awed with the God who gave us the Bible. He does not want you to worship His book. He wants you to cherish it and trust what it says, but it is not the will of the Father for His children to love what He wrote more than we love growing in our relationship with Him. So, He leaves some — questions slow to be answered, and He allows to linger some needs that are delayed in being met.

Yes, He leaves a lot of blank spaces for us. He lovingly, wisely refuses to fill in all the gaps with ahead-of-time information. You are not imagining things – he definitely makes you wait. He allows you *squirming seasons* wherein — ✓ you come to abandon your trust in your own abilities to make things happen or to fix what is presently wrong. Mark it down, **God will fight hard against anything and everything that causes us to embrace any independence from Him.** We typically believe that He wants us strong, and we fail to define the concept of strength in the context of our absolute — dependence upon His love, presence, power, and promises. Perhaps, more — than anything else, this is what I am still figuring out as I go.

When I am weak, then I am strong. In my weakness, His strength is made perfect in me. It is true for you too. The Apostle Paul was made to understand this **(see 2ⁿᵈ Corinthians 12:7-10)**. He, too, figured it out as he went, only fully yielding to this truth about what constitutes real strength when Jesus refused to remove Paul's own personal and painful struggle. Paul called this thing a *thorn* piercing his flesh. Jesus literally told Paul that this thing that made Paul weak was essential to Paul living in the truest of strengths. After wrestling in prayer with Jesus over this, Paul was eventually brought to the place where he surrendered to the astounding grace of God. Sometime after that, Paul saw his thorn in the flesh as something that was not opposing his progress and development as a believer but actually something holy and good that was empowering him in the Spirit. He ended up declaring that he matured to the place where the weakness and struggle he once despised and wanted to go away became something that he boasted in as a treasure because it brought him so much closer to his King.

So, let's understand this:

Everything that crushed Paul's potential self-reliance was a gift from God to him. Truly, Paul's pain became his gain. **Will you dare to entertain the**

thought that everything that has worn down your own self-trust is also a gift? The unanswered questions in your life are a gift from God. That thing that fell apart on you and broke you deeply – can you treat it as a gift from the Father? Those hurts, that abandonment, his or her betrayal of you that was never acknowledged, those slanderous words against you – all of these are things which carved out new places where the Father can inject mercy, grace, wisdom, and victory. That thing which is calling you into the valley for a fight like gargantuan Goliath called out to diminutive David is nothing less than a full-fledged opportunity for you to rely on God like you never have before! Seasons of human loneliness provide space for increased intimacy with the Almighty. Impossible needs require a supernatural resourcing from Heaven – will you believe that there is grace from Him to you in things like this?

Can you see how that, if God gave you everything you needed to know or needed to possess ahead of time, you would likely not press in toward Him in need? There is something within the infinite heart of God that doesn't only want us to operate in what He said in the past **but also what He is saying in present moments.** He likes spending time with you so much that He sets up your life in such a way that you have to enter His presence every day. What He spoke in the past is good and reliable. There will be no conflict between what He once said and is now saying, but He delights for daily intimacy with you. That's why He leaves unanswered questions and unmet needs for us. He likes us near to Him. He doesn't really *send us off for Him*. He calls us to walk alongside Him. The Father is all about proximity and quality time – that is His primary love language. We might possibly be able to serve Him missionally if He gave us all the details ahead of time, but we certainly cannot cultivate deep friendship with Him apart from being in His presence daily.

Our weakness and need, perhaps more than anything else, drive us into His presence. When we stay in rhythm with that pulse of our hearts to come boldly before His throne to find help and obtain mercy in our time of need, something starts to shift inside of us. As that shift occurs, a new thing begins to dawn in our hearts. We find that our daily desire to spend intimate time with the unseen God is no longer primarily driven by our weakness and need. It is now driven **by love**.

We move from being creatures motivated by need, and we enter into being sons and daughters motivated toward Him by love. We want time and intimacy with the Father because we have been made to fall in love with Him as He has proven Himself so good and faithful to us in our training times of weakness and need. We become convinced of His goodness and worth – and who wouldn't want to spend quality time with a God like that?

So, it's all about Him loving us until we love Him back.

It's not about us being strong, competent, or informed.

It's about our dependent trust.

It's about learning who is this eternally good and glorious Father who has made us the object of His immeasurable love.

It's about learning how to live life as an exhale instead of holding our breath as we wait to see how things will play out.

Yes, it's about being loved by Him.

This is the greatest, most treasured thing that I am still happily figuring out as I go.

My prayer is that you are figuring out the same.

Made in the USA
Columbia, SC
09 February 2020

87563810R00107